Syllabus

1. Principles of Solar Energy
2. Solar Energy Utilization
3. Wind Energy
4. Maximum Power Extraction
5. Bio-Mass
6. Geothermal Energy
7. Ocean Energy

Principles of Solar Radiation

Solar Constant : The mean extraterrestrial radiation normal to the solar beam on the outer fringes of the earth's surface is called Solar constant. Its value is approximately $1.353 \ kW/m^2$.

This varies by $\pm 3.4\%$ during the year due to elliptical orbit of the earth.

Extraterrestrial Solar Radiation

The intensity of the Sun's radiation outside the earth's atmosphere is called extraterrestrial radiation & has no diffuse components. The radiations are measured as an average earth-Sun distance on a surface normal to radiation with the help of high flying aircraft, ballons, Satellite etc. The energy flux is called Solar constant & denoted by I_{sc}.

The extraterestrial radiation observed on different days is known as apparent extraterrestrial Solar irradiance & can be calculated on any day of the year using following equation;

$$I_0 = I_{sc} \left[1 + 0.033 \cos \frac{360 n}{365} \right]$$

$n \rightarrow$ No. of days of the year counting January 1 as the first day of the year.

$$I_{sc} = 1.353 \ kW/m^2$$

Terrestrial Solar Radiation

The radiation we receive on the earth surface is called the terrestrial radiation & is nearly 70% of extraterrestrial radiation. The rate of terrestrial energy falling on a unit surface area in W/m^2 is variably referred to as radiation, irradiation, irradiance, insolation or energy flux. Terrestrial radiation varies significantly

1) It varies daily because of earth's rotation around the sun.

2) It changes seasonally because of sun's declination angle, i.e. the angle b/w the sun's rays & the earth's equatorial plane normal to the polar axis.

3) It changes due to spacial changes b/w the sun & the earth, due to elliptical motion of earth.

* The extraterrestrial radiations are attenuated are attenuated by the following:

1) Scattering: A part of a radiation beam is scattered laterally & attenuated by the air molecules, water vapour & dust in the atmosphere. The scattered & diffuse radiation is mostly of shorter wavelengths.

2) Absorption: The solar radiation is absorbed by ozone (O_3), water vapour (H_2O) & CO_2.

Solar Radiation Geometry

The amount of incident beam flux on an inclined surface per unit time per unit area is given as

$$I_N = I \cos \theta_i$$

where I = incident flux of beam radiation

θ_i = angle of incident of beam radiation.

For horizontal surface, $\theta_i = \theta_z$.

<u>Latitude (ϕ)</u>: The latitude is the angular measurement between radial line joining location (observer) to the center of earth & its projection on equatorial plane.

<u>Longitude (L)</u>: It is the angular distance measured from west or east to an observer point on the earth's surface which passes through the prime meridian (Greenwich, England).

<u>Declination Angle (δ)</u> The angle b/w the line joining sun & center of earth & its projection on the equatorial plane is called the declination angle.

$$\delta = 23.45 \sin \frac{(284 + n) \times 360}{365}$$

n = day no. of the year, taking January 1 as 1st day.

Hour angle (ω): It is the angular distance that the earth has rotated in a day to bring the meridian of the sun inline with the meridian of the observer on an equatorial plane.

$$\omega = 15(h-12)$$

h = current time (solar time) of the day.

Altitude angle (α): The solar altitude is the vertical angle between the sun rays & a horizontal surface. At sunset/sunrise the altitude is $0°$ & when the sun is at zenith, the altitude angle is $90°$.

Zenith angle (θ_z): The angle made by sun rays from vertical line passing through the observer is called zenith angle.

Solar azimuth angle: (γ_{sun}) The azimuth angle is the angle made between the projection of sun's rays on the horizontal plane & the line joining South to bar when projection is east of south the angle is +ve & - bot other direction in the northern hemisphere.

Surface azimuth angle (γ): The angle b/w the line due South or north & the projection of normal to inclined surface on a horizontal plane.

Solar wall azimuth angle (α_w): The angle b/w north to inclined plane & projection of sun ray on horizontal plane.

Angle of incident (θ_i): The angle between beam radiation & the normal to inclined surface is known as angle of incident.

Sun angle: The sun angle is a beam of light making angle with the surface of the earth. It determines the area of illumination & intensity of heating.

Solar Time:

Solar time = Standard time + $4(L_{st} - L_{location})$ + Equation of time correction.

where

L_{st} = Standard Longitude of local time zone (country)

$L_{location}$ = Longitude of location/observer in the country

Equation of time given (in minutes) by

$$Equation = 229.2 \times 10^{-6}(75 + 1870 \cos A - 32077 \sin A - 14615 \cos 2A - 40890 \sin 2A)$$

where $A = \dfrac{(n-1)360}{365}$

n = no. of day of the year.

The standard longitude of India is $81° 54'$.

Solar angles on tilted surface:

The angle of incident on tilted surface is expressed as

a) when tilted surface is facing in any direction

$$\cos\theta_i = \cos\theta_z \cos\beta + \sin\theta_z \sin\beta \cos\gamma_{relative}$$

$$\gamma_{relative} = \gamma_{sun} - \gamma_{surf}$$

$$\cos\gamma_{sun} = \frac{\sin\phi \cos\delta \cos\omega - \cos\phi \sin\delta}{\sin\theta_z}$$

$\beta \rightarrow$ tilt angle of surface from horizontal & is taken positive when surface is sloping towards the south direction. &

$$\sin\gamma_{sun} = \frac{\cos\delta \cos\omega}{\sin\theta_z}$$

b) When tilted surface is facing south

$$\Rightarrow \gamma_{surface} = 0$$

c) When surface is horizontal

$$\beta = 0 \ \& \ \theta_i = \theta_z$$

d) When surface is vertical & facing south

$$\gamma = 0 \ \& \ \beta = 0$$

Solar day length:

The time interval b/w two successive passages of sun across the meridian of observer is known as Solar day length.

Irradiance on tilted Surface:

The angle relation on tilted surface is shown in below figure. If the direct beam (I_b) & diffuse (I_d) radiation are known on the horizontal surface, the radiation flux can be calculated on inclined surface by using Lieu & Jorden method for converting the radiation on horizontal surface to tilted surface.

The total radiation on tilted surface is expressed as

$$I(t)_{tilted} = \underset{(Beam)}{I(b)_t} + \underset{(Diffuse)}{I(d)_t} + \underset{(Reflected)}{I(de)_t}$$

$$I(b)_t = I(b)\cos\theta_i$$
$$I(b)_h = I(b)\cos\theta_z$$

$t \rightarrow$ tilted

$h \rightarrow$ horizontal

$$\frac{I(b)_t}{I(b)_h} = \frac{\cos\theta_i}{\cos\theta_z} = R_b \ (\text{tilt factor})$$

$$\boxed{I(b)_t = R_b \, I(b)_h}$$

lly

$$I(d)_t = I(d)_h \left(\frac{1+\cos\beta}{2}\right)$$

$$I(de)_t = I(t)_h \, \rho \left(\frac{1-\cos\beta}{2}\right)$$

ρ is albedo

$\Rightarrow$

$$I(t)_{tilted} = R_b \, I(b)_h + I(d)_h \left(\frac{1+\cos\beta}{2}\right) + I(t)_h \, \rho \left(\frac{1-\cos\beta}{2}\right)$$

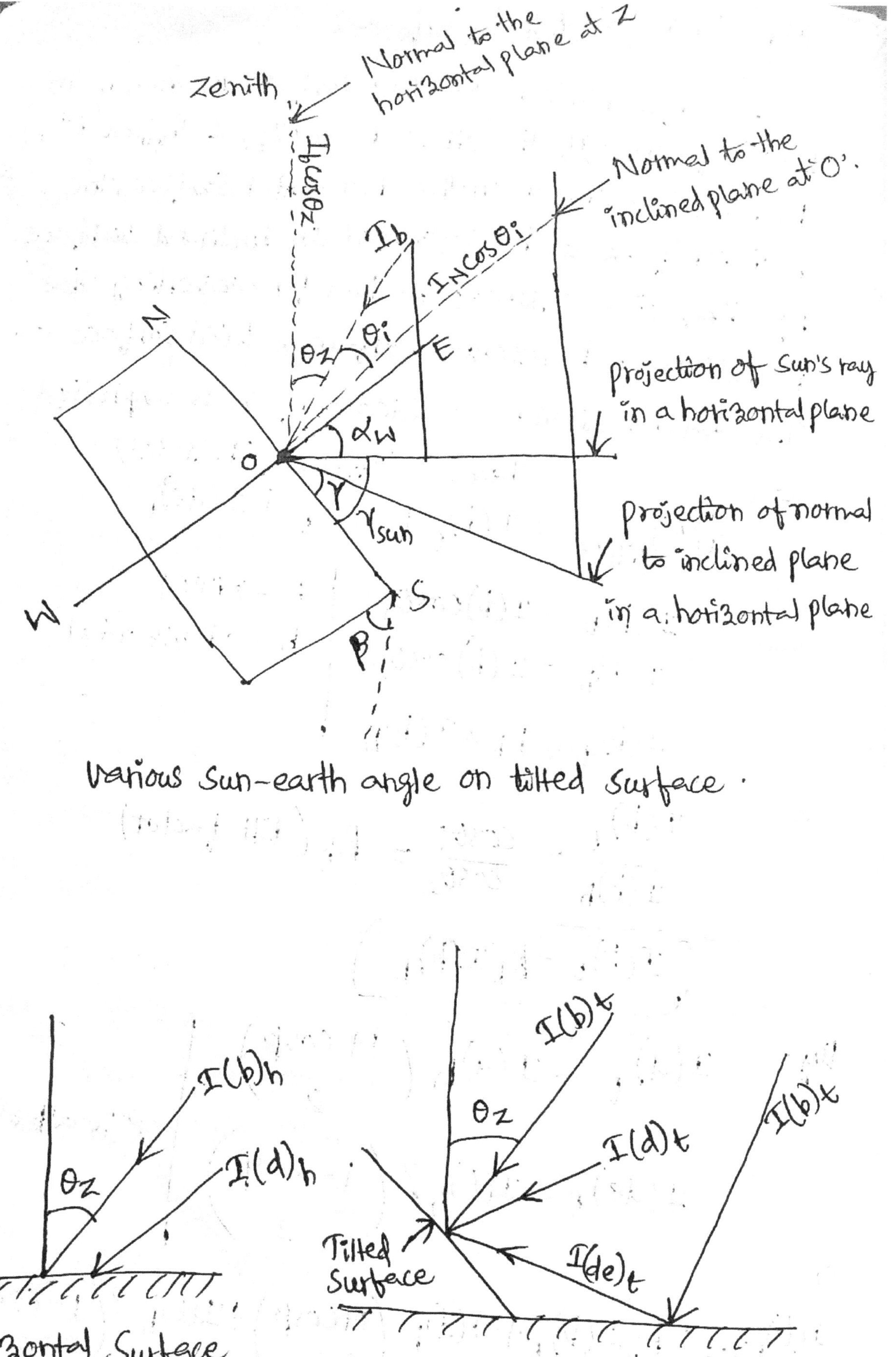

Various Sun-earth angle on tilted surface.

Optimum tilt angle of the Surface:

* The solar thermal system fixed at one position doesn't track the sun & needs to be fixed at an angle for getting the average maximum solar radiation for better performance. It is observed that average tilt angle for the surface facing due south at northern hemisphere is taken as latitude (ϕ) of location. However how much it should be tilted is found to be dependant on the nature of collection of energy demanded in a year (vary with seasons) & latitude of the place. Therefore optimum tilt for the year is taken as, ~~-----~~ $\phi \pm 15°$.

NOTE: In winter season the sun is at lower position & more tilt angle $(\phi \pm 15°)$ is preferred to lower down the reflection & applicable in space heating.

    Similarly in summer the sun is at vertical overhead, most of the time & lower angle $(\phi - 15°)$ is preferred to maximize the energy collection as applicable in refrigeration. However overall performa -nce is found better at tilt angle, latitude of location (ϕ).

Solar Radiation Data

*) Radiation : It is the Average cumulative daily solar
radiation on a horizontal surface in MJ/m^2 per day
are available for different locations.

1) Altitude Angle (Solar altitude) (α) ⎫
⎬ Refer in.
2) Zenith angle (θ_z) ⎬ previous
⎭ Section.
3) Solar Azimuthal angle (γ_s)

4) Clearness Index (C_i)

  All the effects of Solar angles, Scattering, absorp-
-tion, cloudiness may be combined in one parameter
called the clearness Index. C_i is the ratio of average
radiation on a horizontal surface for a given period to
the average extraterrestrial radiation for the same
period.

Measurements of Solar Radiations

  The total radiation is the sum of both the beam
& diffuse components. The following measurements are
made

1) Beam radiation on a horizontal surface:

  A pyrheliometer is used to measure the beam
radiation on a horizontal Surface. It is a small telescope
mounted on a drive mechanism & follows the sun through
out the day.

2) Diffuse radiations on a horizontal surface

A pyranometer with a shade ring is used to measure the diffuse radiation on a horizontal surface.

3) Total radiation on a horizontal surface

A pyranometer without a shade ring is used to measure the total or global radiations.

4) Sunshine duration

A sunshine recorder is used to measure the hours of bright sunshine during the course of a day. A lens burns a trace on a card when exposed to the sun. The length of the trace directly measures the duration of bright sunshine.

5) Beam Radiation on a normal surface

The total radiation received by a surface normal to the beam radiation is more than that on a horizontal surface. Therefore, a radiation collecting surface would be more effective when held perpendicular to the direction of the sun rays. The collector surface should track the sun by changing angle of installation.

2. Solar collection

2. Solar Energy collection

Solar collectors :

Solar collectors are used to collect the solar energy & convert the incident radiations into thermal energy by absorbing them. This heat is extracted by flowing fluid (air or water or mixture with antifreeze) in the tube of the collector for further utilization in different applications. They are classified as -

1) Non - concentrating collectors
2) Concentrating collectors

Non - concentrating collectors

1) Flat plate collectors : It is the most important part of any solar thermal energy system. It is simplest in design & both direct & diffuse radiations are absorbed by collector & converted into useful heat. These collectors are suitable for heating to temperature below 100°C.

Advantages :

1) It utilises the both the beam as well as diffuse radiation for heating
2) Requires less maintanance.

Disadvantages :

1) Large heat losses by conduction & radiation because of large area.
2) No tracking of Sun
3) Low water temperature is achieved.

<u>CONSTRUCTION :</u>

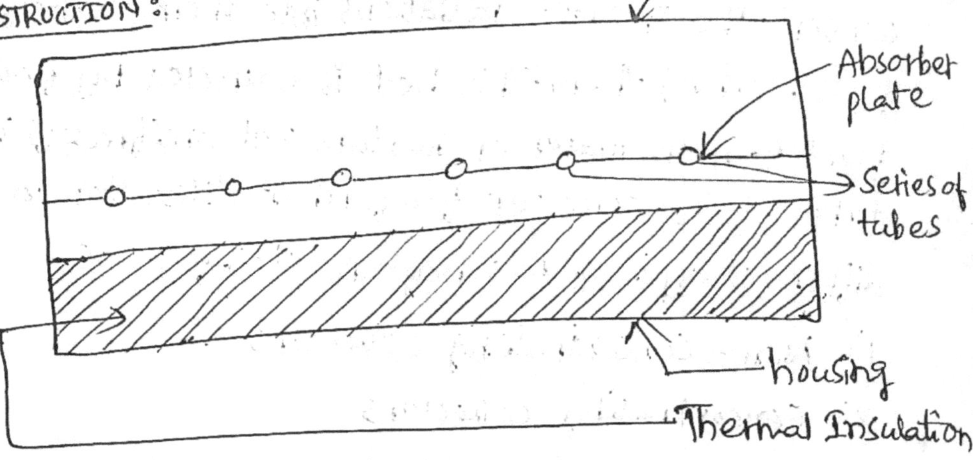

a) <u>Insulated Box</u> : The rectangular box is made of thin G.I Sheet & is insulated from sides & bottom using glass or mineral wool of thickness 5 to 8 cm to reduce losses from conduction to back & side wall. The box is titled at due South & a tilt angle depends on the latitude of location. The face area of the collector box is kept b/w 1 to 2 m^2.

b) <u>Transparent cover</u> : This allows solar energy to pass through & reduces the convective heat losses from the absorber plate through air space. The transparent tampered glass

The concentrating collectors are classified as

1) **FPC with Reflectors**: The mirrors are placed as reflecting surface to concentrate more radiations on FPC absorber. The fluid temperature is higher by 30°c than achieved in FPC. These collectors utilize direct & diffuse radiation.

2) **Lens focussing type**: The fresnel lenses are used to concentrate the radiation at its focus. The lower side of lenses is grooved so that radiation concentrates on a focus line.

3) **Compound parabolic Collectors**: These collectors are line focussing type. The compound parabolic collectors have two parabolic surfaces to concentrate the solar radiation to the absorber placed at bottom. These collectors have high concentration ratio & concentrator is moving to track the sun.

4) **Cylindrical parabolic collectors**: The troughs concent-rate sunlight onto a receiver tube, placed along the focal line of the trough. The temperature at the absorber tube is obtained at nearly 400°C. The absorber in these collectors is moving to receive the reflected radiations by reflector, while the concentrators (trough) remains fixed. Because of its parabolic shape, it can focus the sun at 30 to 100 times its normal intensity (concentration ratio) on a

Concentrating collectors:

These collectors are used for medium $(100-300^\circ c)$ & high temperature (above $300^\circ c$) applications such as steam production for the generation of electricity. The temperature is achieved at absorber because of reflecti-ng arrangement provided for concentrating the radiation at required location using mirrors & lenses. These collectors are best suited to places having more number of clear days in a year.

The area of absorber is kept less than the aper-ture through which the radiation passes, to concentrate the solar flux. These collectors require tracking to follow the sun because of optical system. The tracki-ng rate depends on the degree of concentration ratio & needs frequent adjustment for system having high concentration ratio. The efficiency of these collectors lies b/w $50-70\%$. The collectors need more maintanance the flat plate collectors, because of its optical system. The concentrating collectors are classified on the basis of reflector used; concentration ratio & tracking method adopted & a shown in fig. below:

As the liquid circulates through the tubes, it absorbs the heat from absorber plate of the collectors. The heated liquid then enters in a heat exchanger or is added directly to the conventional system. If the heat removal rate is slow then the losses from collector will increase because of rise of high temperature of collector & will lower the efficiency. Flat plate solar collector are less efficient in cold weather than in warm weather.

cover is placed on top of rectangular box to trap the solar energy & sealed by rubber gaskets to prevent the leakage of hot air. ~~The~~ It is made of plastic/glass but glass is most favourable because of its transmitta- -nce & low surface degradation.

c) **Absorber plate**: It intercepts & absorbs the solar energy. The absorber plate is made of copper, alumini- -um or steel & is in the thickness of 1 to 2mm. It is the most important part of collector along with the tubes or ducts passing the liquid or air to be heated. The plate absorbs the maximum solar radia- -tion incident on it through glazing (cover plate) & transfers the heat to the tubes in contact with ~~maximum~~ minimum heat losses to atmosphere.

d) **Tubes**: The plate is attached to a series of parallel tubes or one serpentine tube through which water or other liquid passes. The tubes are made of copper, aluminium or steel in the diameter 1 to 1.5 cm & are brazed, soldered on top/bottom of the absorber plate.

Removal of heat: These systems are best suited to applications that require low temperatures. Once the heat is absorbed on the absorber plate it must be removed fast & delivered to the place of storage for further use

receiver. The heat transfer medium carries the heat at one central place for further utilization.

5) **Parabolic Dish Collector**: The collectors have mirror like reflectors & an absorber at the focal point. These collectors are point focussing type. The concentrating ratio of these collectors is 100 & temperature of the receiver can reach up to 2000°C. These collectors have higher efficiency for converting solar energy to electricity in the small power plant. In some systems, a heat engine, such as a Stirling engine, is connected to the receiver to generate electricity.

6) **Center receiver type (Solar power Tower)**

These collectors are used to collect the large solar energy at one point. This system uses 100-10000 of flat tracking mirrors called heliostats to reflect the solar energy to central receiver mounted on tower as shown in fig. The losses of energy from the system are minimized as solar energy is being directly transferred by reflection from the heliostats to a single receiver where the sun's rays heat a fluid to produce steam.

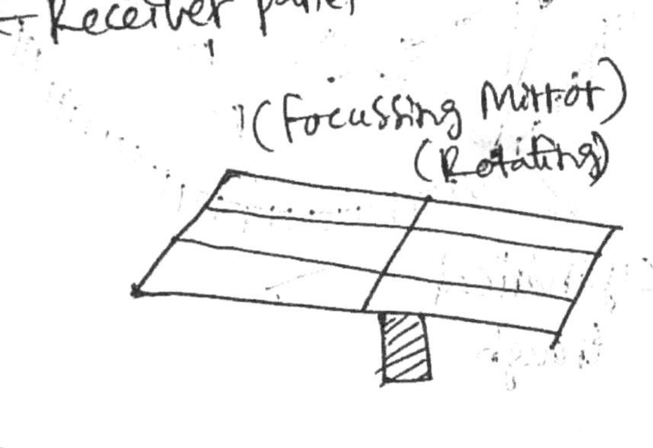

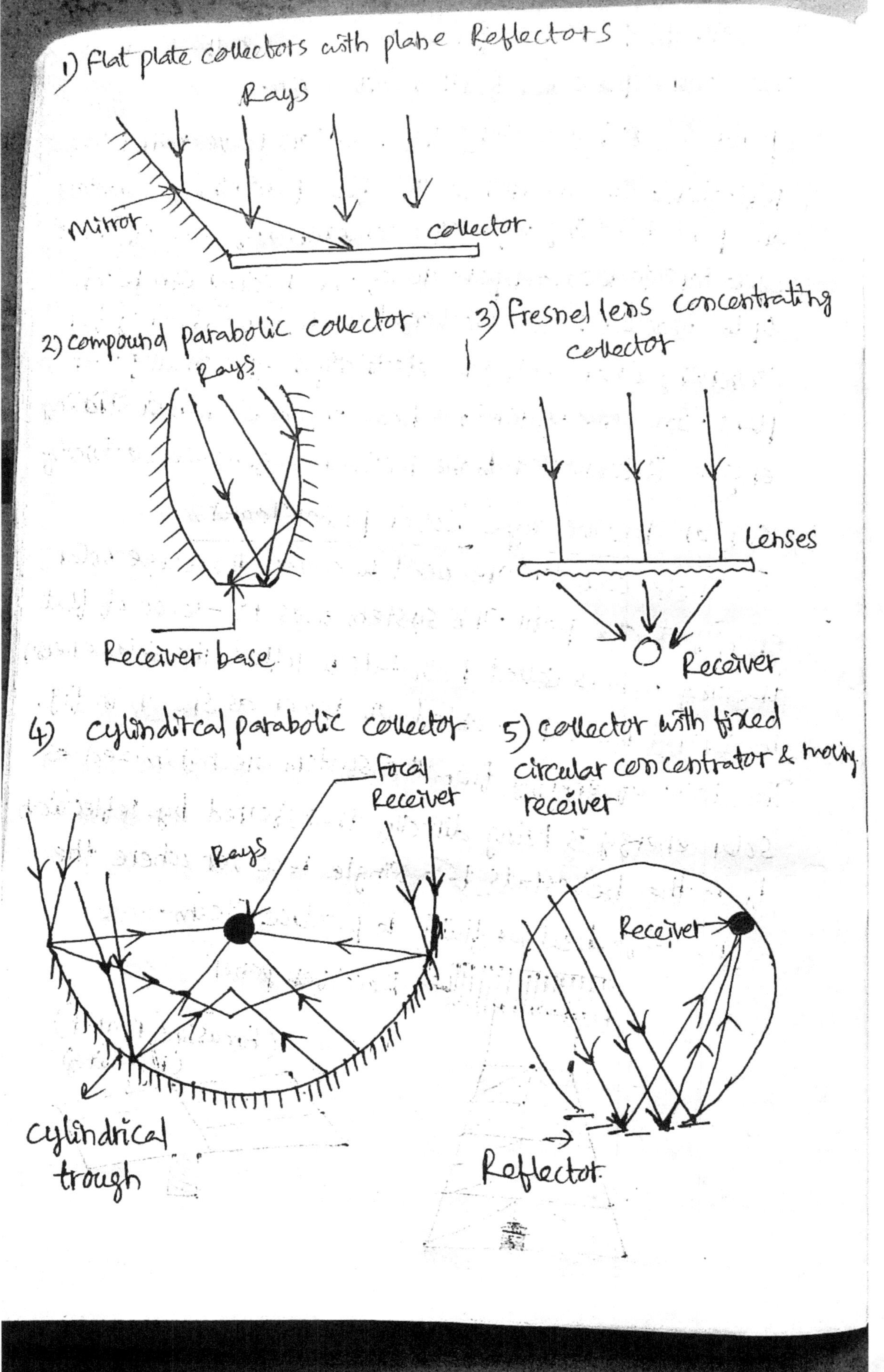

1) Flat plate collectors with plane Reflectors
Rays
Mirror
collector
2) compound parabolic collector
Rays
Receiver base
3) Fresnel lens concentrating collector
Lenses
Receiver
4) cylindrical parabolic collector
focal Receiver
Rays
cylindrical trough
5) collector with fixed circular concentrator & moving receiver
Receiver
Reflector

6) parabolic dish collector

7) central Receiver Heliostats

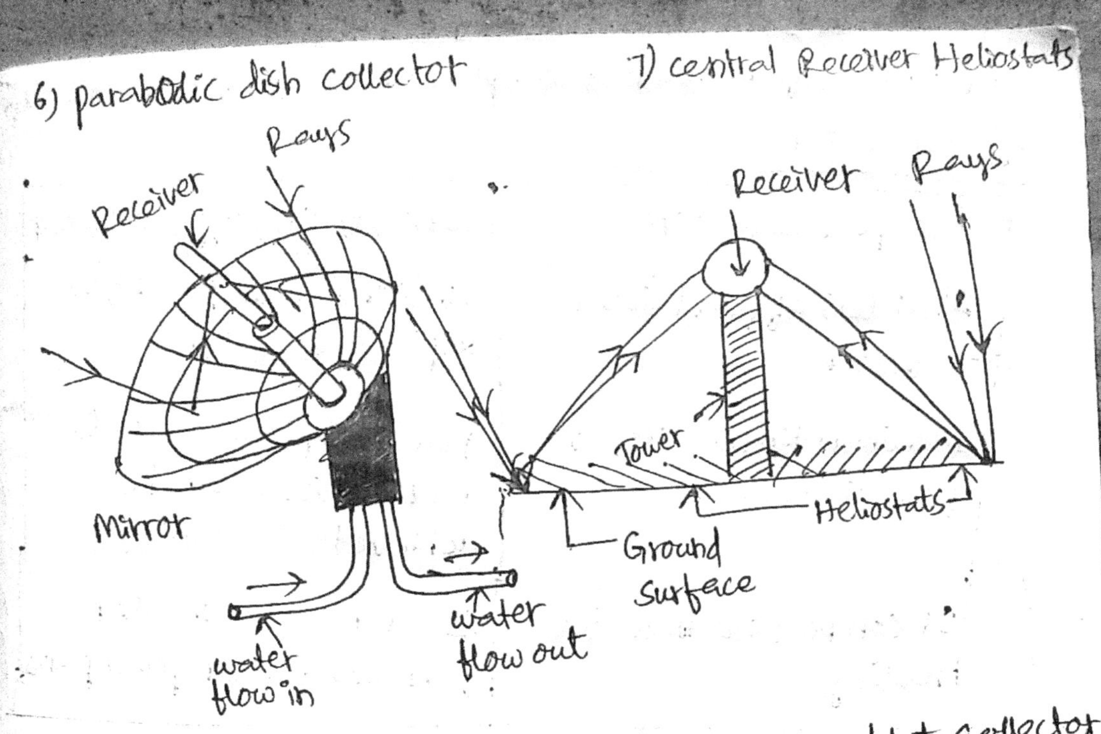

Advantages of concentrating collector over flat collector

1) The size of the absorber can be reduced that gives high concentratio ratio

2) Thermal losses are less than FPC. However small losses occur in the concentrating collector because of its optical system as well as by reflection, absorption by mirrors & lenses.

3) The efficiency increases at high temperatures.

4) In these collectors the area intercepting the solar radiation is greater than the absorber area.

5) These collectors are used for high temperature applications.

6) Reflectors can cost less per unit area than flatplat collectors.

6) parabolic dish collector   7) central Receiver Heliostats

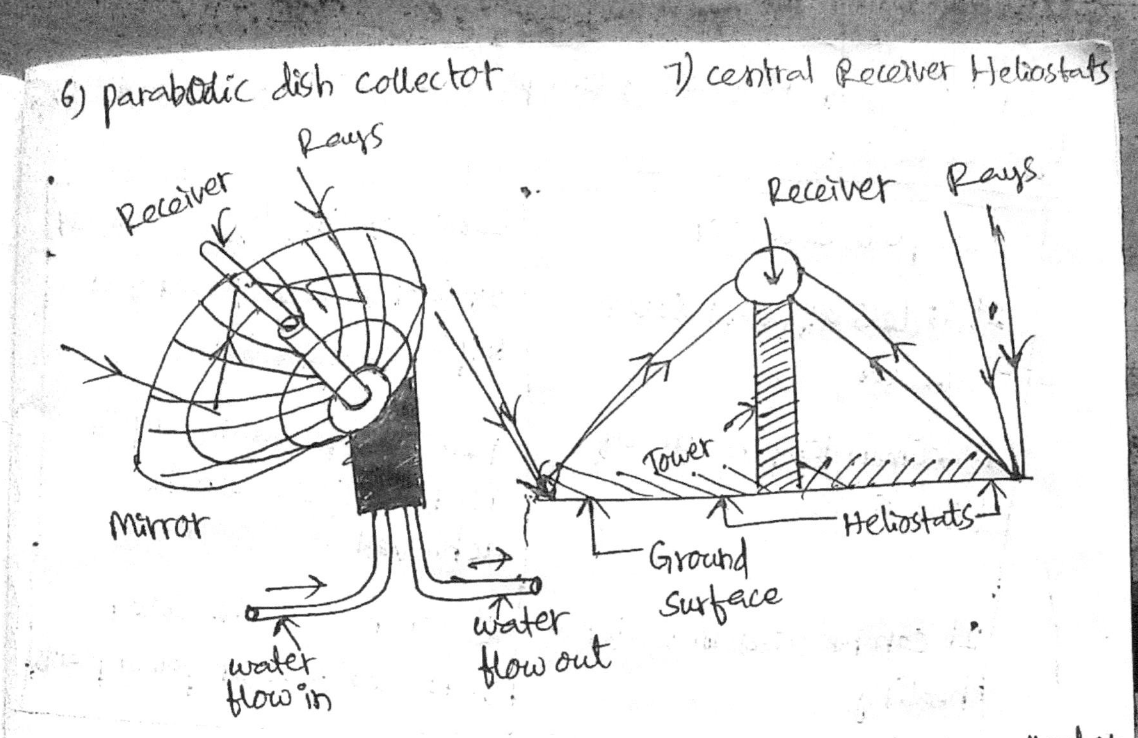

Advantages of concentrating collector over flat collector

1) The Size of the absorber can be reduced that gives high concentratio ratio

2) Thermal losses are less than FPC. However small losses occur in the concentrating collector because of its optical system as well as by reflection, absorption by mirrors & Lenses.

3) The efficiency increases at high temperatures.

4) In these collectors the area intercepting the solar radiation is greater than the absorber area.

5) These collectors are used for high temperature applica-tions.

6) Reflectors can cost less per unit area than flatplate collectors.

Comparision of between Flat plate collector & concentrating type collector :

Flat plate collector	concentrating type collector
It is less efficient solar collector	It is the most powerful type of collector
Maximum temperature of fluid is 300°c	Fluid temperatures upto around 5000°c can be achieved
It can be used in water heating	It can be used in solar furnaces & solar power plants

Comparision of performance of different collectors :

Type of collector	Effective optical efficiency	Effective heat loss coefficient $(W/m^2\text{-}K)$	Operating Temperature $(°c)$	Cost $\$/m^2$
Flatplate collector with no cover	0.9	15-20	30	120-170
Flatplate collector with single cover	0.8	35-40	<100	300-500
Evacuated tube collector	0.7	1.5-1.8	<250	700-1000
Parabolic trough collector	0.8	0.2-0.7	400	~700

Thermal Analysis of collectors :

Here the thermal analysis of the collectors is presented. The two major types of collectors, i-e flat plate & concentrating are examined. The basic para-meter to consider is the collector thermal efficiency. This is defined as

" The ratio of the useful energy delivered to the energy incident on the collector aperture. The incident solar flux consist of direct & diffuse radiation".

While FPC can collect both, concentrating collectors can only utilise direct radiation if the concentration ratio is greater than 10.

Flat plate collectors performance Evaluation :

The useful heat output of a flat plate collector is given by :

$$Q_c = A\left[I_c F_R (\tau\alpha)_e - F_R U_c (T_{in} - T_a)\right] (W)$$

where

A = surface area of collector or absorber (m^2)

I_c = Intensity of solar radiation incident on the collector (W/m^2)

F_R = Heat removal factor of the collector

$(\tau\alpha)_e$ = Effective product of transmissibility τ of the transparent cover & absorptinty α of the absorber

U_c = overall heat loss coefficient of collector (W/m^2)

T_{in} = Fluid inlet temperature $(^\circ c)$

T_a = Ambient air temperature $(^\circ c)$

The efficiency of the solar collector is defined as the ratio of the useful heat output of the collector & the solar energy flux incident on the collector.

$$\eta_c = \frac{Q_c}{A I_c}$$

$$= \frac{F_R (\tau\alpha)_e - F_R U_c (T_{in} - T_a)}{I_c}$$

let $\dfrac{(T_{in} - T_a)}{I_c} = X$

The performance curve of a collector can be plotted between η_c & X.

PT = parabolic trough concentrator

ETC = Evacuated Tube collector

FP = flat plate collector

The following parameters can be found out from the performance curves.

1) At $x = 0$, $\eta_c = F_R(\tau\alpha)_e$ = Effective optical efficiency.

2) The value of effective overall heat loss coefficient $F_R U_c$.

The outlet temperature of the fluid from the collector can be found out as

$$T_{out} = T_{in} + \frac{Q_c}{\dot{m} C_p} \quad (^\circ C)$$

where T_{in} = Inlet temperature of fluid $(^\circ C)$
   Q_c = Useful heat output of collector (W)
   $\dot{m}$ = mass flow rate of fluid $(kg/s.)$
   C_p = Specific heat of fluid $(J/kg-k)$

The stagnation temperature is the temperature of the observer when there is no fluid flow.

$$\therefore Q_c = 0 \ \& \ \eta_c = 0 \ \& \ if \ T_{in} = T_{stag}$$

$$\therefore T_{stag} = T_a + \frac{I_c F_R(\tau\alpha)_e}{(F_R U_c)}$$

Concentrating collectors performance Evaluation :

The useful heat output,

$$\boxed{Q_c = F_R A_a \left[I_{bc} \eta_{opt} - \left(\frac{U_c}{C} \right) \right] (T_{in} - T_a)} \ (W)$$

where

Solar radiation passes through the glass envelope tube & projects onto the absorber plate. The absorber plate absorbs solar radiation & converts it into heat & then transfers heat to the heat pipe. The heat vaporizes a working fluid inside the evaporator section. The vapour moves up to the condenser section, & the latent heat of the vapour is released to a cooler surface of the condenser section during condensation of working fluid. The liquid returns to the evapourator section by gravity. The entire process then repeats itself.

2) Direct flow ETC:

The direct flow evacuated tube is very similar to the heat-pipe evacuated tube in appearance, dimensions & configuration, except concentric pipes instead of the heat pipe. Direct flow ETC is mainly composed of inner pipe, outer pipe, absorber plate, glass envelope tube, metal sealing cover, getter & other

The direct-flow ETC consists of evacuated tubes, manifold, insulation box & other accessories as shown in fig. The heat transfer fluid circulates into the inner pipe & returns through the outer pipe into the heating circuit, while directly removing the heat from the absorber plate.

Evacuated Tube collectors (ETC)

ETCs can be classified according to the materials used for making the absorbers. Thus there are metal absorbers & glass absorbers. ETC with ~~glass~~ metal absorbers, ~~because they~~ possess special advantages: their ability to withstand high pressure & to endure thermal shock, both of which are very necessary for most solar thermal systems.

There are two types of ETCS
1) Heat pipe ETC
2) Direct flow ETC.

Heat pipe ETC: It consists of evacuated tubes, a manifold, an insulation box & other accessories as shown in fig.

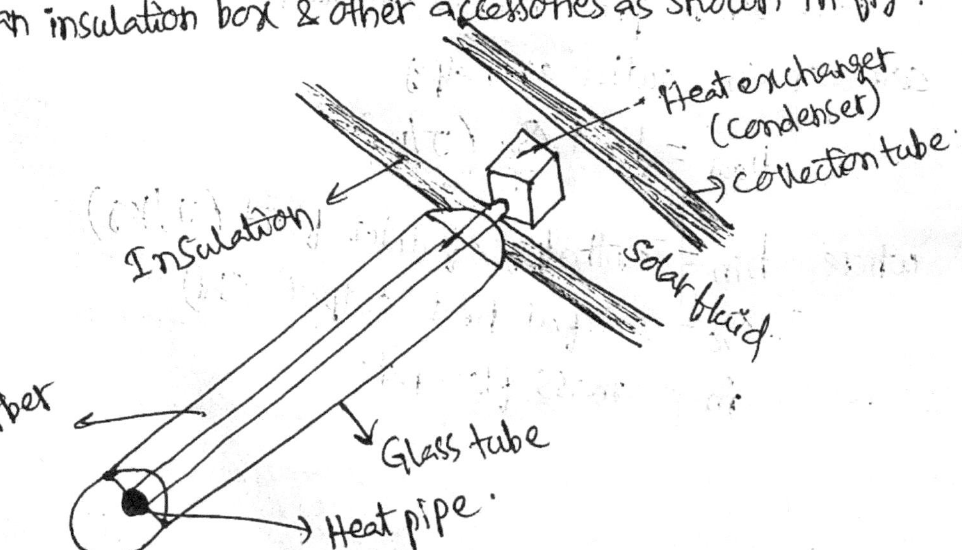

Efficiency of the collector,

$$\eta_c = \frac{Q_c}{A_a I_{bc}}$$

$$\eta_c = F_R \eta_{opt} - \left(\frac{F_R U_c}{C I_{bc}}\right)(T_{in} - T_a)$$

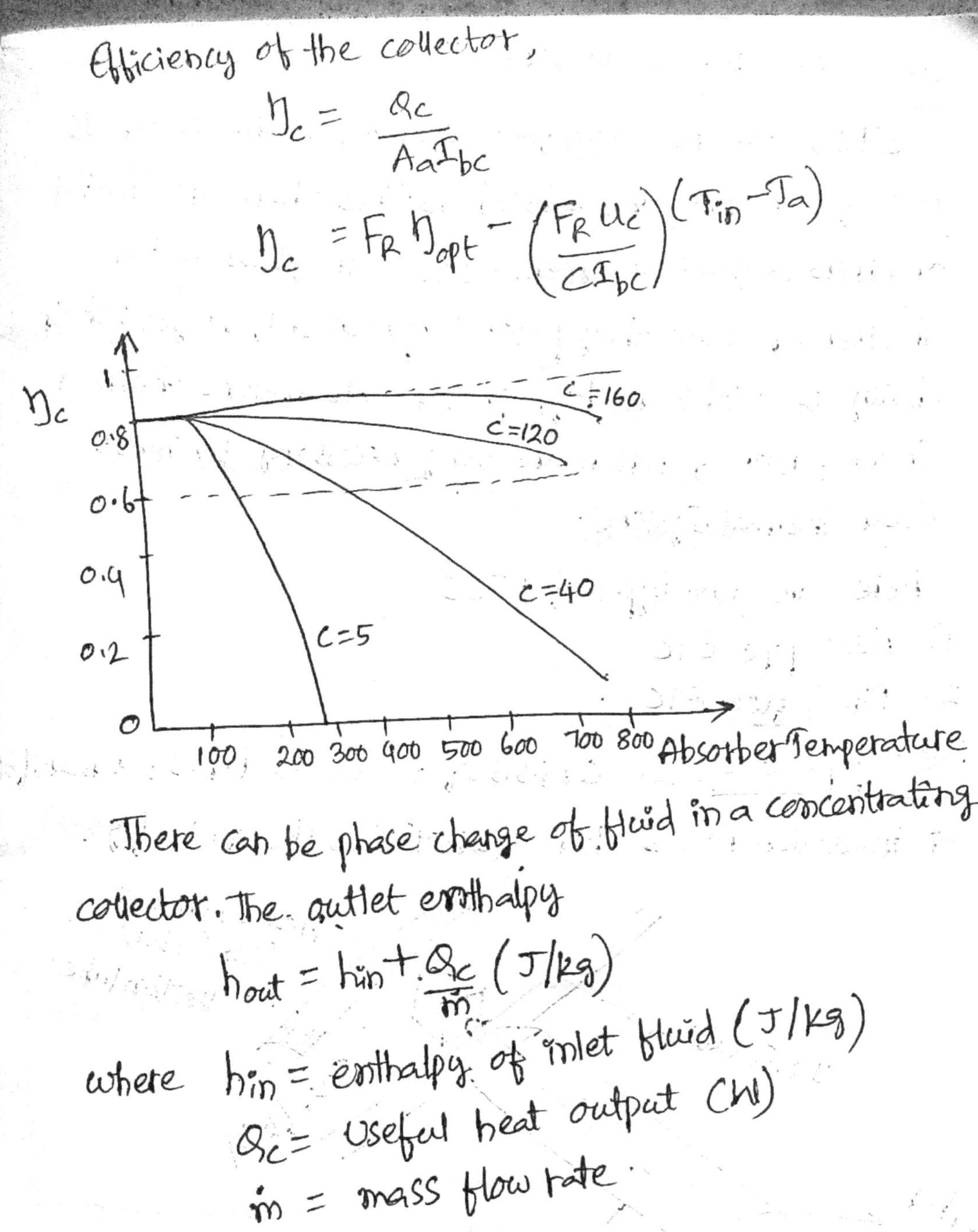

There can be phase change of fluid in a concentrating collector. The outlet enthalpy

$$h_{out} = h_{in} + \frac{Q_c}{\dot{m}} \quad (J/kg)$$

where h_{in} = enthalpy of inlet fluid (J/kg)

Q_c = useful heat output (W)

$\dot{m}$ = mass flow rate

F_R = Heat Removal factor of the collector

A_a = Unshaded aparture area

I_{bc} = Intensity of beam radiation on aparture of the collector

η_{opt} = optical efficiency of the collector (W/m^2-k)

C = concentration ratio of the collector

T_{in} = Inlet temperature of fluid $(^\circ c)$

T_a = Ambient temperature $(^\circ c)$

optical efficiency:

It is the ratio of solar radiation absorbed & the beam radiation on the concentrator

$$\eta_{opt} = \eta_{opt(^\circ c)} \, C_{opt}$$
$$= \rho \, \gamma \, \tau \, \alpha_a \, C_{opt}$$

where

$\eta_{opt(0^\circ c)}$ = optical efficiency at 0° incident angle of beam

C_{opt} = Correction factor for deviation from 0°

ρ = Reflectivity of mirror

γ = Intercept factor

τ = Transmittivity of the cover (if available)

α_a = Absorptivity of absorber

Sun
Insulation
Cold water supply
Hot water return
Absorber
outer glass tube
Vaccum
Inner glass tube
Inner copper tube

Advantages of Heat pipe ETC:

1) Resistance to freezing
2) Quick start
3) Low heat losses
4) Resistance to high pressure
5) Resistance to thermal shock.

Advantages of direct-flow ETC

1) Higher thermal efficiency
2) Flexible installation
3) Resistance to high pressure
4) Resistance to thermal shock

Pyrheliometer :

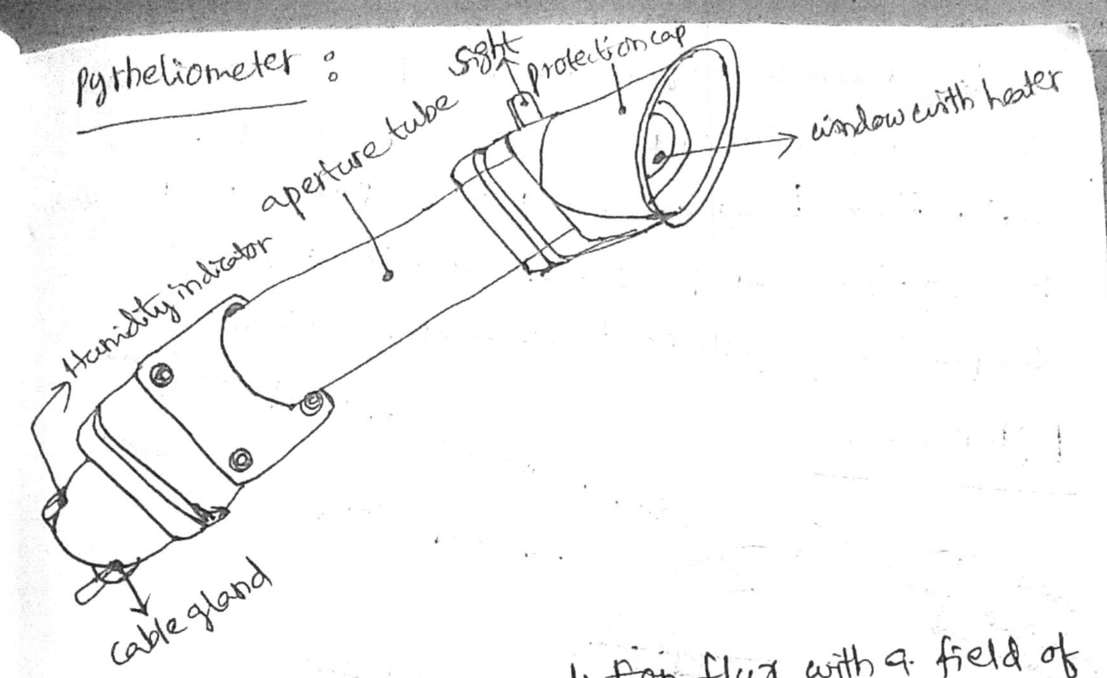

It measures the Solar radiation flux with a field of view of 5 degrees. The solar radiation spectrum extends roughly from 300 to 2800 nm. It follows that a pyrhelio meter should cover that spectrum with a spectral sensi-tivity i-e as "flat" as possible.

For correct measurement it should be pointed at the sun. In order to attain the proper spectral characteristics, a pyrheliometer's main components are:

1) A thermopile sensor with a black coating. This sensor absorbs all solar radiation, has a flat spectrum from visible light to Infra-red & has a near-perfect cosine response.

2) A quartz window. This window limits the spectral response from 200 to 4000 nm. Another function of the window is that it shields the thermopile sensor from convection.

the black coating on the thermopile sensor absorbs the solar radiation. This radiation is converted to heat, which flows through the sensor to the pyrheliometer housing. The thermopile sensor generates a voltage output i.e. proportional to the solar radiation.

Pyranometer

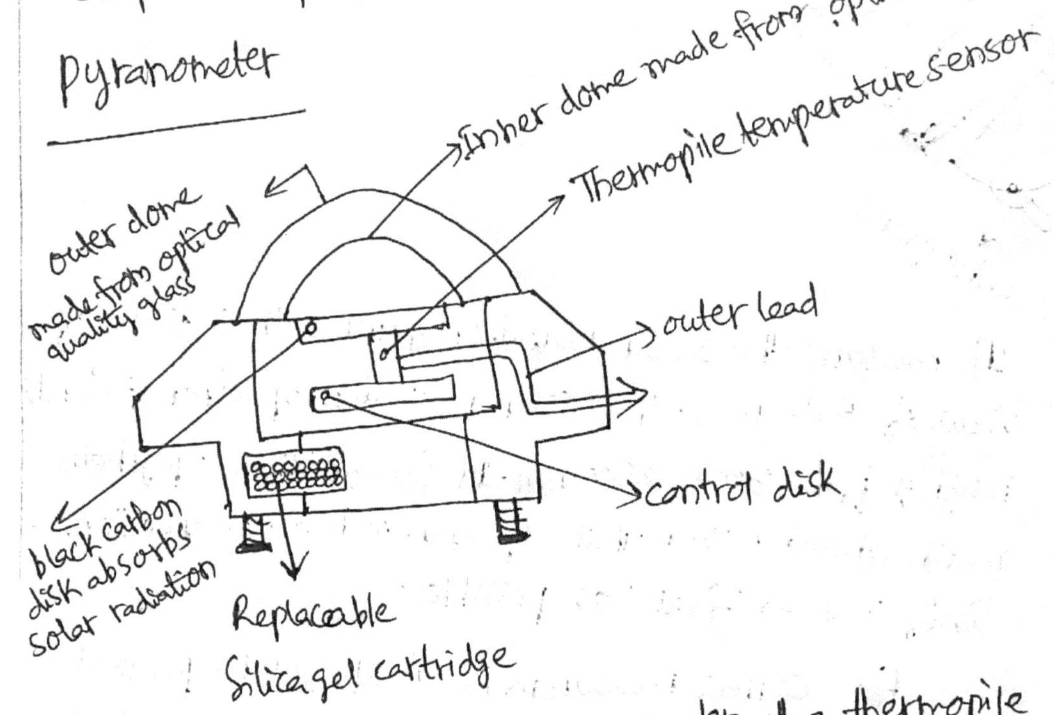

When sunlight falls on a pyranometer, the thermopile sensor produces a proportional response typically in 30 seconds or less. the more sunlight, the hotter the sensor gets & the greater the electric current it generates. The thermopile is designed to be precisely linear & also has a directional response. it produces maximum output when the sun is directly overhead (at midday) & zero output when the sun is on the horizon (at dawn or dusk). This is called a cosine response (or cosine correction), because the electrical signal from the pyranometer varies with the cosine of the angle b/w the Sun's rays & the vertical.

Methods of Harnessing Solar Energy

1) **PV System (photo voltaic Systems):** These are panels made from materials that, when exposed to sunlight, use heat & light to shake electrons & create an electric current in a process called the photovoltaic effect.

2) **Solar water Heating:** Solar collectors are usually rectangular chambers with multiple small tubes called flat plate collectors, which circulate water or another fluid.

3) **Passive Solar energy:** passive solar heating & lighting can be achieved both directly & indirectly through different methods.

4) **Solar thermal electricity:** Solar energy can be concentrated to heat water & run turbines to produce clean electricity. There are

5) **Solar Heating & Cooling:** For offices & larger buildings, solar energy can be more efficiently harnessed, as compared to houses & smaller premises. On a larger scale, even parabolic trough collectors can be used for space heating & solar water heating in place of traditional methods.

Direct Radiation : is also known as "beam radiation or direct beam radiation". It is used to describe solar radiation travelling on a straight line from the sun down to the surface of the earth.

Diffuse Radiation : It describes the sun light that has been scattered by molecules & particles in the atmosphere but that has still made it down to the surface of the earth.

Direct radiation has a definite direction but diffuse radiation is just going any which way.

Scattering & Reflection :

Scattering : It is a process where interaction b/w the two colliding particles occurs in the process of diversion of a path of a particle or a wave.

Reflection : It is a process of diversion of a path of a particle or a wave due to a non-interaction collision.

UNIT-3 Wind Energy

Types of Wind turbine

Like old wind mills, today's wind machines use blades to utilize the wind's kinetic energy. Windmills works because they slow down the speed of the wind simultaneously as the wind flows over the airfoil shaped blades causing lift, like the effect on airplane wings & cause them to turn. The blades are connected to shaft that turns an electric generator to produce electricity. The wind passes through the rotor blades & gives the circumferential torque to rotate the shaft.

With new wind mills there is still the problem when the wind is not blowing. The other types of powerplants must be used as a stand by to make electricity. There are two types of wind machines used today to harness the wind energy.

i) Horizontal-axis wind machines

ii) Vertical-axis wind machines

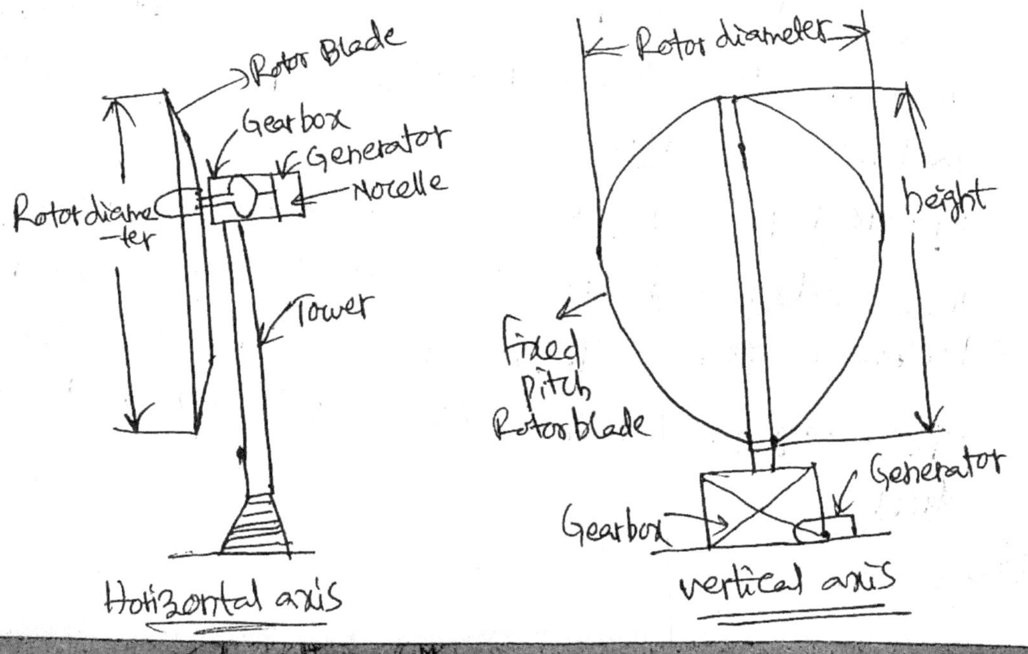

A 150 – 200W vertical turbine will be able to cover 10 to 15%. of a household's electricity use. Wind turbines have around 4 to 5 years payback time & over 10 years life span.

On the basis of power available from wind, the wind power plants are grouped in three categories.

i) Small Size: These wind turbines have $P_{o/p} = 10 - 50$ KW & rotor diameter of 1 – 16 m.

ii) Medium Size: $P_{o/p} = 50 - 500$ KW, Rotor dia = 16 – 50 m

iii) Large Size: $P_{o/p} = 500 - 5000$ KW & Rotor dia = 50 – 130 m

Horizontal Axis:

Most wind mills are the horizontal-axis type & are more popular. A typical horizontal wind machine stands as tall as a 20-storey building. The horizontal axis wind turbines have one, two, three or multi rotor blades with span of 60 m across. The large wind machines in the world have blades longer than a football field. One wind machine rates from 15 KW to 3 MW & can produce 1.5 to 4 million kWh of electricity in a year which is sufficient for 150 – 400 homes. There are different types of horizontal axis wind machines like mono blade, twin blade & three blade types. The propellers of the machine are two types.

Upward type rotor: The blades are slanted in such a way that wind approaches from front side, to drive the rotor.

Downward type rotor: The design is such that the wind is approaching from back side (nackle side) & moves towards the front.

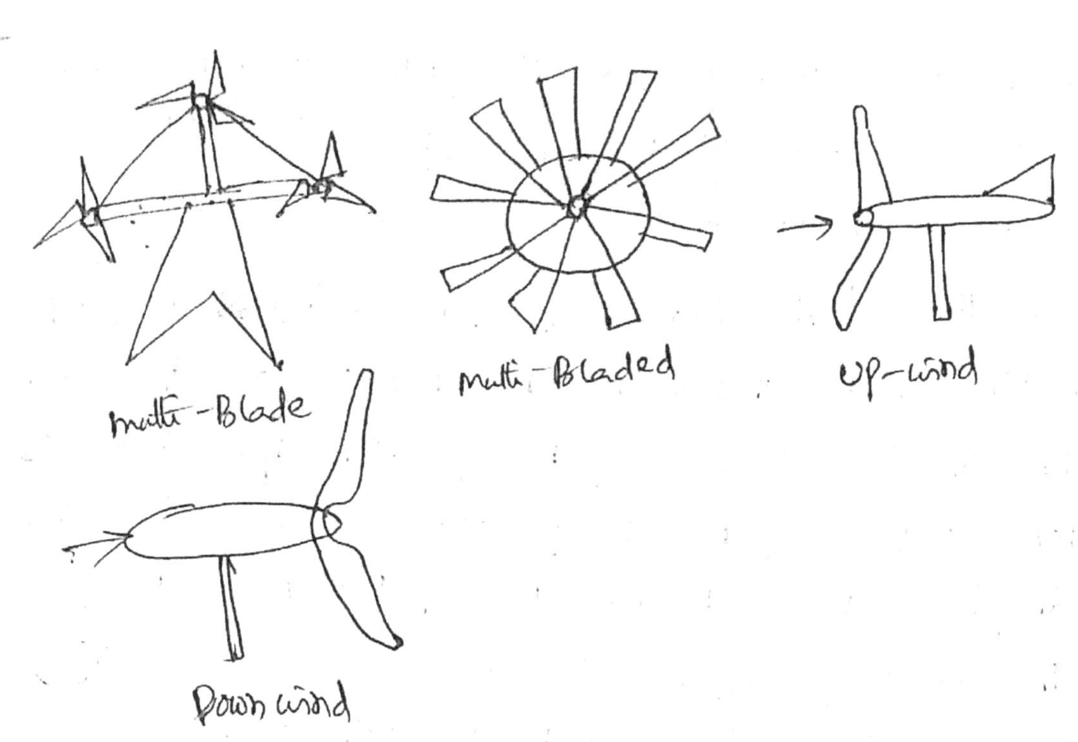

Vertical- axis.

These turbines are mounted on ground level & have blades that go from top to bottom & look like egg beaters. The typical vertical axis machine stands 30 m tall & 15 m wide. vertical axis wind machines are nearly 5% of the wind machines used today. These machines are very large in size from 4MW & above.

The most popular vertical axis machines are:

a) Savonious type: The rotors of these turbines are 's' shaped & supported at top & bottom by two circular plates as shown in fig. The two curved blades are fixed on central pipe & are free to rotate. The air strikes on concave side, circulating through centre of rotor & glides over the convex surface of the other blade. These turbines suffer from disadvantage that when the convex surface of turbine is facing the wind the speed of turbine slows down. The two blade rotor of turbine was modi -fied to four blade rotor, so that one concave surface will always be there to allow the air flow in whatever may be the wind direction. The tip to speed ratio of turbine is 1-2 & is nearly 15-30% efficient.

These turbines are useful for grinding grain, pumping water, & many other tasks; but are not good for genera-ting electricity because of low rpm. The rpm above 1000 is generally best for producing electricity. However drag based vertical machines usually turn below 100 rpm.

The advantages of this rotor are:

1) low wind speed is sufficient to operate the machine
2) pitch & yaw control not required
3) Generator can be mounted on ground
4) Low system cost

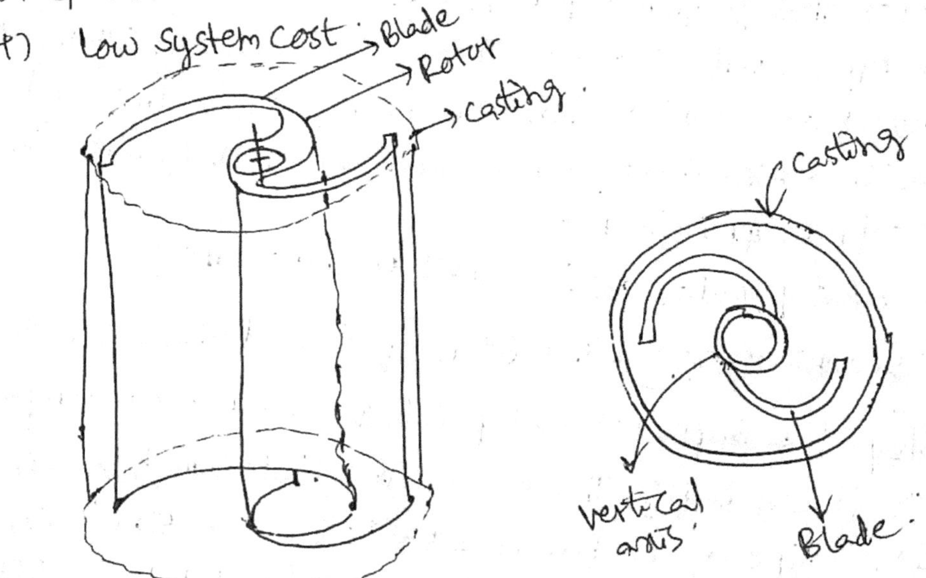

B) <u>Darrius wind machine</u>: The only vertical axis turbine which has ever been manufactured commercially, is named after the french engineer Georges Darrieus. He patented the design in 1931 & many machines were installed

in USA & Canada by 1980. The Darrius wind turbine.
shown consists of 2 or 3 airfoil C-shaped rotor blades,
fixed on vertical axial pipe, that looks a like an egg beater.
The rotor rotates on two bearing placed on top & bottom of
pipe, with wind blowing from any direction. These turbi-
-nes suffer a problem of stalling when wind speed is very
high. The wind turbine is anchored on ground by wire
ropes & generator is mounted on ground. The rotor is not
self starting & needs auxiliary starter. These turbines
are available in sizes 4 MW, 10 MW & 14 MW capacity
with efficiency of 35-40%. These airfoil shaped blades
are difficult to manufacture, transport & install. To
overcome this problem H type turbine blade is being
developed.

Advantages :

1) The generator, gear box etc. are placed on the ground.
2) No need of yaw mechanism to turn the rotor against
   the wind.

Disadvantages :

1) Wind speeds are very low close to ground level, so
   although you may save a tower, your wind speeds will
   be very low on the lower part of your rotor.
2) The overall efficiency of the vertical axis machines is low.
3) The m/c is not self-starting.
4) The m/c may need guy wires to hold it up
5) Blades are difficult to manufacture, transport & install.

parts of wind turbine :
____

a) Anemometer : measures wind speed

b) Blades :

c) Generator :

d) Controller : Starts up the m/c at wind speeds about 4·5 m/s &
                                    shuts off at about 22 m/s.

e) Gearbox : Gears are step planetary spur gear system & connect
the low speed shaft to the high-speed shaft to increase the
rotational speed of the gear box , from about 50 rpm upto
1800 rpm as required by most of generators to produce
electricity.

f) High speed shaft :

g) Low speed shaft :

h) Brake

i) Nacelle : placed at the top of the tower & contains the gear
box , low & high speed shafts, generator, controller & brake.

j) pitch : Blades are turned, pitched in & out of the wind speed
to control the rotor speed & keep the rotor turning at required
rpm to produce electricity.

k) Rotor

l) Tower

m) wind vane : It measures wind direction & communicates with
the yaw drive to orient the turbine properly w·r t the wind.

n) Yaw drive : It is used to keep the rotor always facing into
the wind direction as the wind direction changes & is
electromechanically driven. Downward turbines don't require a
yaw drive.

o) Yaw motor : It powers yaw drive.

Controls of wind turbine :

As wind speed varies, the speed of the generator varies & produces fluctuations in the electricity. The problems can be solved by following approach.

i) To have constant speed turbines where the blades adjust the pitch, by turning slightly to the side, to adjust the wind speeds.

ii) To use variable-speed turbines, where the blades & gene-rator change speed with the wind & power controls fix the fluctuations of the electrical output.

iii) To use low speed generators.

A) **Teething Control :** It is provided with mono & twin blade type horizontal axis turbine to prevent failure because of vibration (fatigue) during orientation of necelle. The axis of the turbine gets positioned in such a way that the propeller blades revolve in slanting plane at higher speed. The slants get reduced at low speed & get increased at higher speed.

B) **Yaw Control :** It is provided to position the nacelle automatically in the direction of wind with the help of hydraulic mechanism & continuously orient the rotor in the direction of wind. The axis is oriented in such a way that rotor swept area is perpendicular to the wind flowing either in upward or downward direction.

c) __Pitch control__ : The blade tips are adjusted automatically to provide feathering action. This reduces the speed & power of turbine to match with the generator speed - The pitch angle has wide control between 0-30°.

Wind power :

Let 'm' be the mass flow rate of air moving with velocity 'V' through opening provided at any time. The kinetic energy associated with this moving air is

$$E = \frac{1}{2} m v^2$$

This is max. power associated within the wind. following figure shows the motion of wind through the opening of area (A) flowing with velocity (V). The discharge rate (Q') of air through the opening at point 1 & 2 is given as

$$Q = A \times V$$

Mass flow rate (kg/s) of air through the opening,

$$m = \rho A V$$

$$E = \frac{1}{2} \rho A V V^2 = \frac{1}{2} \rho \frac{\pi}{4} D^2 \times V^3$$

$(\because$ circular area of cross section$)$

$$\therefore E_{max,wind} = \frac{\pi}{8} \rho D^2 V^3$$

Inlet
$\vec{A}$ ↑D Exit

Instantaneous power of wind $(E_i) = \frac{1}{2} \rho A V_i^3$ &

Average power available from wind for a specified period is taken as

$$\bar{E} = \frac{1}{2} \rho A \bar{V}^3$$

$\bar{V} \rightarrow$ Average velocity
$V_i \rightarrow$ Instantaneous velocity

The above power contained in the flowing wind is not practi-cally extracted by aerogenerator & depends upon the wind speed, turbine type, & spillage losses etc. The spillage loss occurs between the blades as the air spills through the gap B/w the blades. So &

The power developed in aerogenerator = power coefficient × Power available in the wind.

$$E_T = \eta \times E_{max, wind}$$

Performance characteristics:

Wind speed - power characteristics

Turbine Siting:

As a general rule, wind generators are practical where the average wind speed is more than $4.5 \, m/s$. The sites are pre-selected on basis of a wind data & validated with wind measurements. It is necessary to consider technical, environmental, social, economic & other factors before installing the wind turbine.

wind velocity	<$4.4 \, m/s$	$4.5 - 5.4 \, m/s$	$5.5 - 6.7 \, m/s$	>$6.7 \, m/s$
performance	poor	marginal	Good	Excellent

The main criteria for site selections are:

i) The area should be open & away from cities & buildings etc.

ii) Wind should be blowing uniformly throughout the year.

iii) The proposed altitude is to be selected by taking average wind speed data.

iv) Ground surface should be stable.

v) To minimize the transmission losses the wind power should be near the consumers.

vi) The erection land should have low cost.

Different wind sites selected for erection of wind turbine are:

A) On shore (land): Onshore turbine installations are generally 3 kms or more from the nearest shoreline. The hill or ridge causes the wind to accelerate as it is forced over it. Wind farm sits can sometimes be highly controversial, particularly as the hill top, having substantial bird life. The local residents of such potential sites have strongly opposed the installation of the wind farms.

B) **Near-Shore** : Near shore turbine installations are generally considered to be inside a zone that is on land within 3 kms of a shore & on water within 10km of land. wind speeds in these zones share wind speed characteristics of both onshore wind & offshore wind. Winds at sea level carry somewhat more energy than winds of the same speed in mountaineous areas because of the air at sea level is denser & having advantages with both sea & land breeze.

c) **Offshore** : offshore resources experience mean wind speeds about 90% greater than those on land, so offshore resources could contribute about 7 times more energy than land. offshore sites have higher energy yield than on-shore sites, & are generally not visible from the shore even on the clearest days.

Understanding coefficient of power (C_p) & Betz limit :

`$C_p$` is a measurement of how efficiently the wind turbine converts the energy in the wind into electricity.

$$C_p = \frac{\text{Electricity produced by wind turbine}}{\text{Total energy available in the wind}}.$$

Betz Crytena :

Albert Betz was a german physicist who calcalated that no wind turbine could convert more than 59.3% of the kinetic energy of the wind into mechanical energy turning a rotor. This is known as the Betz limit, & is the theoritical maximum coeff. of power for any wind turbine.

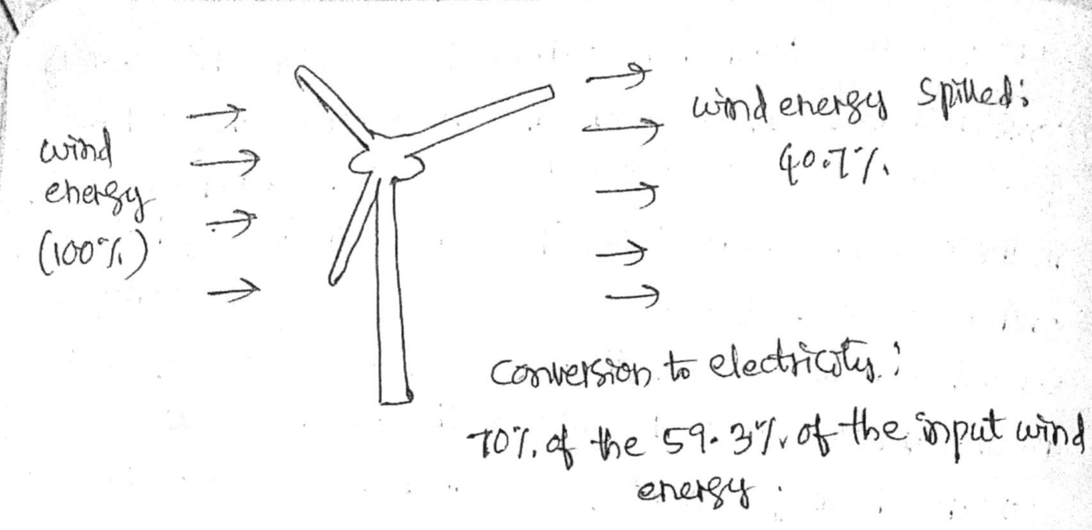

Cp of the turbine = 0.7 × 0.59 = 0.41. So this wind turbine converts 41% of the available wind energy into electricity. This is actually a pretty good coefficient of power. Good wind turbines generally fall in the 35-45% range.

Capacity factor (C_F) of wind turbine: It is the average power generated divided by the rated peak power if it is operated at 100% of time i.e. It is how much electricity a power plant actually produces compared to how much it would produce if it operated at full name plate capacity 100% of the time.

UNIT-IV : Maximum Power Extraction :

Maximum power point tracking for wind

A unique limitation of energy conversion systems such as wind & solar is their inability to track peak power production efficiently at varying wind speeds & solar insulation respectively. This has led to control algorithms referred to as MPPT algorithms. These aids wind & solar energy conversion systems in extracting maximum available power for a given wind & solar resource.

Physics of Energy extraction from wind

$$\text{wind power} = P_0 = \frac{1}{2} \rho A V^3 \ (watts)$$

$\rho \rightarrow$ air density (kg/m^3)
$V \rightarrow$ wind speed

The power in the wind can't be completely converted to mechanical energy of a wind turbine. The theoritical maximum of energy extraction from wind was discovered by Betz & is written as:

$$P_0 = \frac{1}{2} \rho A V^3 C_p = \frac{1}{2} \rho A V^3 (0.59)$$

According to Betz, even if no losses occurred a wind turbine could utilize only 59% of the wind power.

Variable Speed wind turbine

Original models of wind turbines were fixed speed turbines;

i.e the rotor speed was a constant for all wind speeds. The tip speed ratio for a wind turbine is given by this;

$$TSR = \frac{\text{linear speed of blade outermost trip}}{\text{free upstream wind velocity}}$$

$$TSR = \frac{\omega \cdot R}{V}$$

$\omega \to$ rotor speed (rad/s) ; $R \to$ length of a blade.
$V \to$ wind speed.

For a fixed speed wind turbine, the value of the tip-speed ratio is only changed by wind speed variations. In reference to a $C_p - \lambda$ graph, which illustrates the relationship b/w Tip speed ratio & efficiency, it is evident that only one value of λ yields the highest efficiency. This was why variable speed wind turbines were developed.

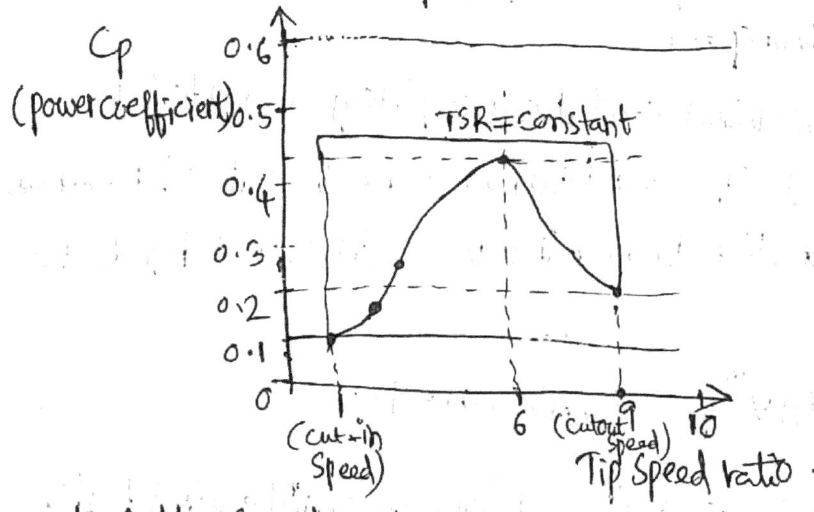

Variable speed configurations provide the ability to control the rotor speed as they often have a power electronic converter stage between the turbine & grid as shown in fig. which allows the wind turbine system to operate constantly near to its optimum tip-speed ratio.

all possible conditions so that the maximum available power is always obtained.

Equivalent circuit of a Solar cell :

$$I = I_L - I_0 \left(e^{\frac{q(V-IR_S)}{AkT}} - 1 \right) - \left(\frac{V - IR_S}{R_{SH}} \right)$$

where $I \rightarrow$ Solar cell output current

     $V \rightarrow$ Solar cell output voltage

     $I_0 \rightarrow$ dark Saturation current

     $q \rightarrow$ charge of an electron, $A \rightarrow$ Diode quality factor.

     $k \rightarrow$ Boltzmann constant, $T \rightarrow$ Absolute Temperature

     $R_S, R_{SH} \rightarrow$ Series & Shunt Resistances of Solar cell

$\underline{R_S}$: It is the resistance offered by the contacts & the bulk semi conductor material of the Solar cell.

$\underline{R_{SH}}$: It is related to the non ideal nature of the p-n junction & the presence of impurities near the edges of the cell that provide a short circuit path around the junction.

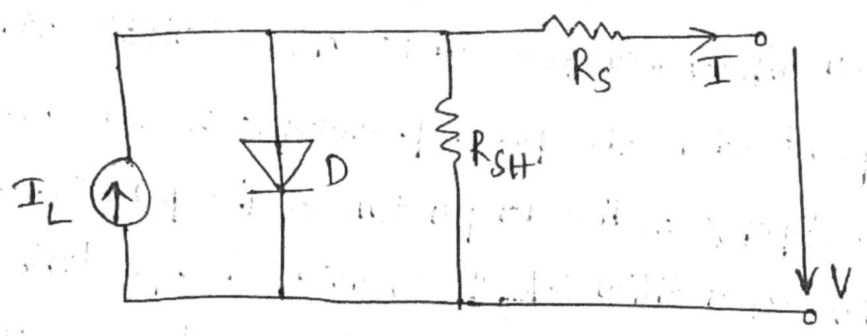

If we neglect R_{sh} :

$$I \approx n_p I_L - n_p I_0 \left(e^{\frac{q(V-IR_S)}{AkT n_S}} - 1 \right)$$

MPPT for PV-Solar power System

The efficiency of a PV plant is affected mainly by three factors: The efficiency of the inverter (15-g PV panel (in commercial PV panels it is between 8-15%.), the efficiency of the inverter (95-98%.) & the efficiency of the MPPT algorithm (>98%.). Improving the efficiency of PV panel & the inverter is not easy as it depends on the technology available, it may require better components, which can increase drastically the cost of the installation. Instead improving the tracking of the maximum power point with new control algorithms is easier, not expensive & can be done even in plants which are already in use by updating their control algorithms, which would lead to an immediate increase in PV power generation & consequently a reduction in its price.

MPPT algorithms are necessary because PV arrays have a non linear voltage-current characteristic with a unique point where the power produced is maximum. This point depends on the temperature of the panels & on the irradiance conditions. Both conditions change during the day & are also different depending on the season of the year. Furthermore, irradiance can change rapidly due to changing atmospheric conditions such as clouds.

It is very important to track the MPP accurately under

2) Tip Speed Ratio (TSR) : This method tries to modify the rotational speed of generator so as to maintain an optimum TSR. The limitation of this method is that wind speed needs to be known along with the turbine rotational speed measurements. This too adds to the system cost.

3) Power Signal feedback : PSF method uses a reference power, which is the maximum power at that particular wind speed. This in itself presents an issue, as the prior knowledge of the wind turbine characteristics & wind speed measurements is required. Once the reference power is obtained from the power curve for a particular wind speed, a comparision with the present power yield is done. The error produced then drives a PI control algorithm.

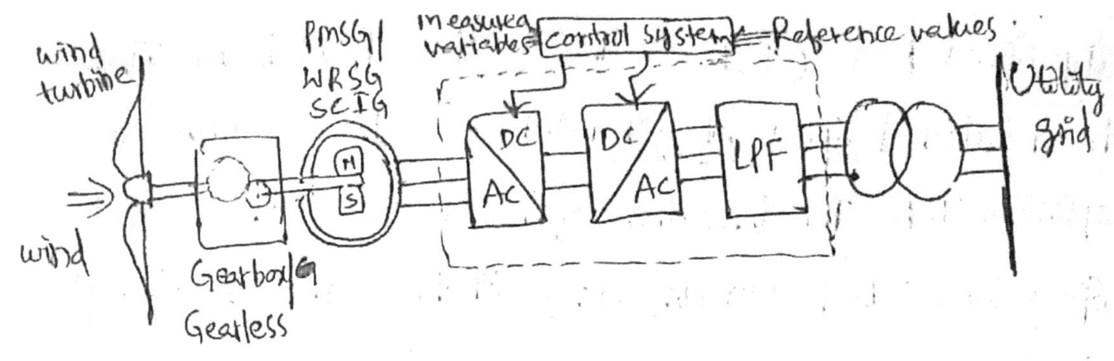

MPPT Algorithms

1) **Hill climb Search (HCS) method (or) Perturb & observe method:**

It makes use of the inverted U shaped graph b/w power & rotor speed. As there is a definite peak power corresponding to a particular rotor speed, the algorithms compares the present power at an instant to the power obtained at the previous step.

If the power is found to be increasing, then the duty cycle of the gating pulse applied to the converter switch are increased to drive the operating point more towards the peak power. If power is found to be decreasing, then duty cycle will be reduced.

Advantages: Simplicity & Independence from wind turbine characteristics

Disadvantages: Inability to track MPPT in cases of abruptly varying wind conditions.

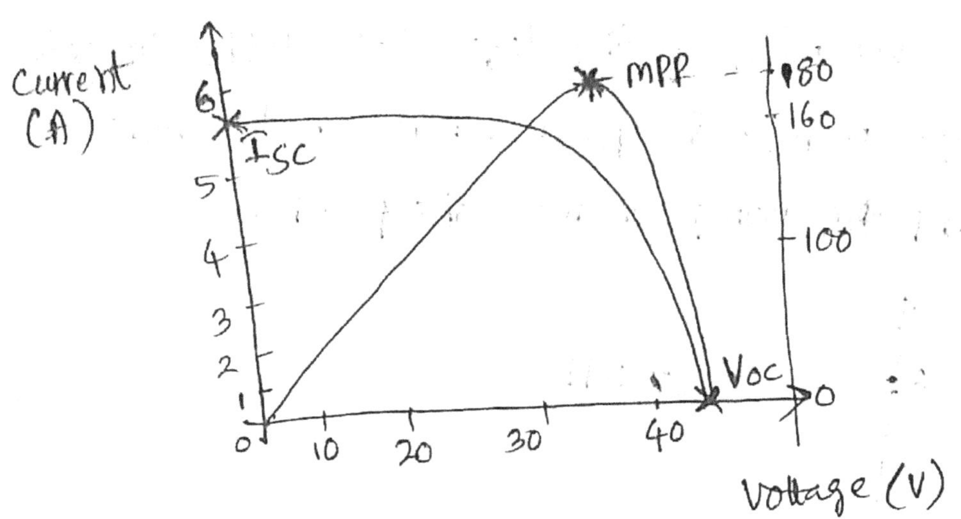

MPPT algorithms:

Hill climb methods:

1) perturb & observe:

The P&O algorithm is called "hill-climbing", but both names refer to the same algorithm depending on how it is implemented. Hill climbing involves a perturbation on the duty cycle of the power converter & P&O a perturbation in the operating voltage of the DC link between the PV array & the power converter. In the case of the hill climbing, perturbing the duty cycle of the power converter implies implying the voltage of the DC link between the PV array & the power converter, so both names refer to the same technique.

In this method, the sign of the last perturbation & the sign of the last increment in the power are used to decide what the next perturbation should be.

As can be seen in fig. on the left of the MPP, incrementing the voltage increases the power whereas on the right, decrementing the voltage increases the power.

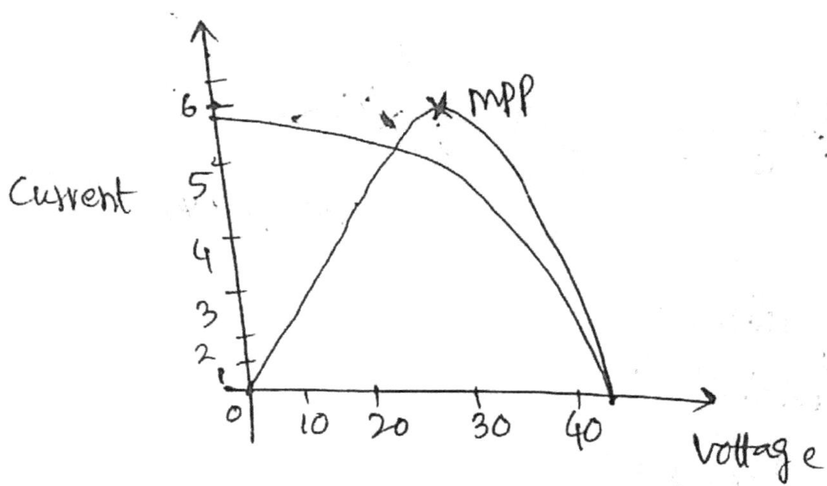

If there is an increment in the power, the perturbation should be kept in the same direction & if the power decreases, then the next perturbation should be in opposite direction. Based on these facts, the algorithm is implemented. The process is repeated untill the MPP is reached.

2) Incremental Conductance

The incremental conductance algorithm is based on the fact that the slope of the curve power vs. voltage (current) of the PV module is zero at the MPP, positive (negative) on the left of it & negative (positive) on the right, as seen in fig.

* $\Delta V/\Delta P = 0$ ($\Delta I/\Delta P = 0$) at the MPP
* $\Delta V/\Delta P > 0$ on the left
* $\Delta V/\Delta P < 0$ on the right

By comparing the increment of the power vs the incre-ment of the voltage (current) between two consecutive samples, the change in the mpp voltage can be determined.

Algorithm flow chart (InCond Scheme)

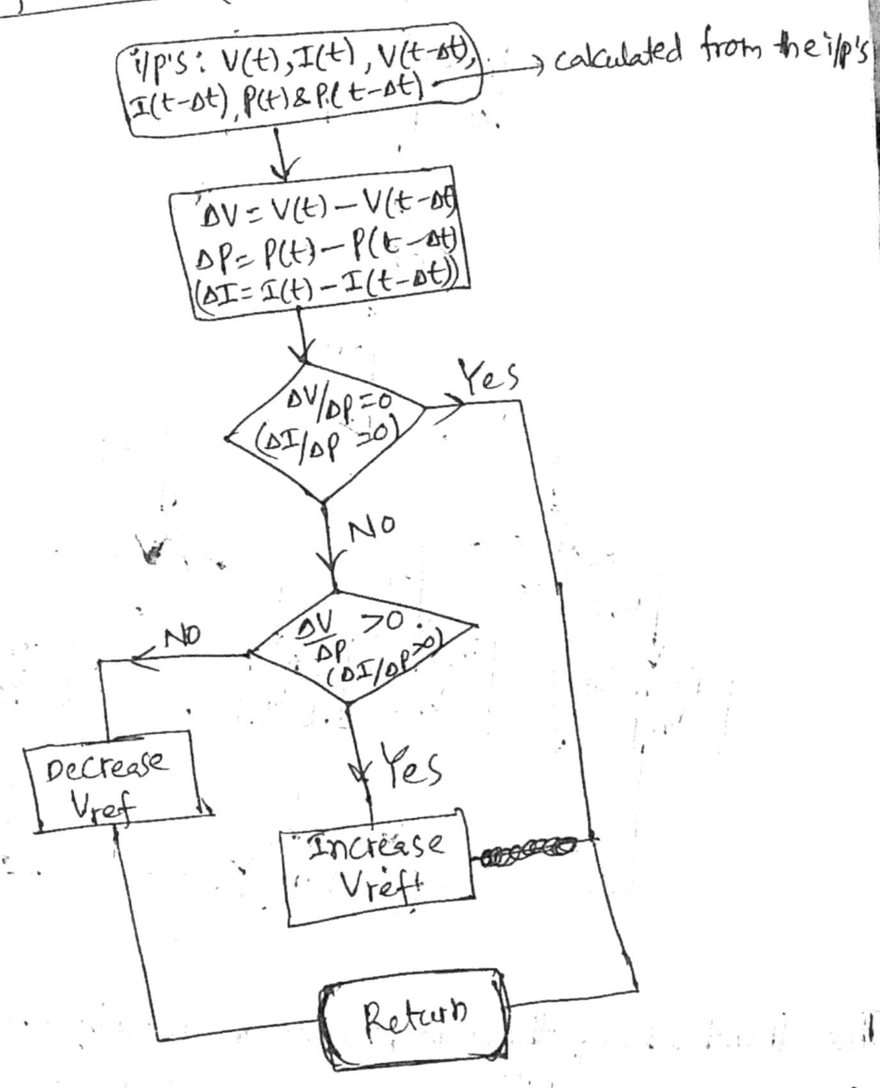

In both P&O & InCond schemes, how fast the mpp is reached depends on the size of the increment of the reference voltage.

Algorithm flow chart (P&O scheme)

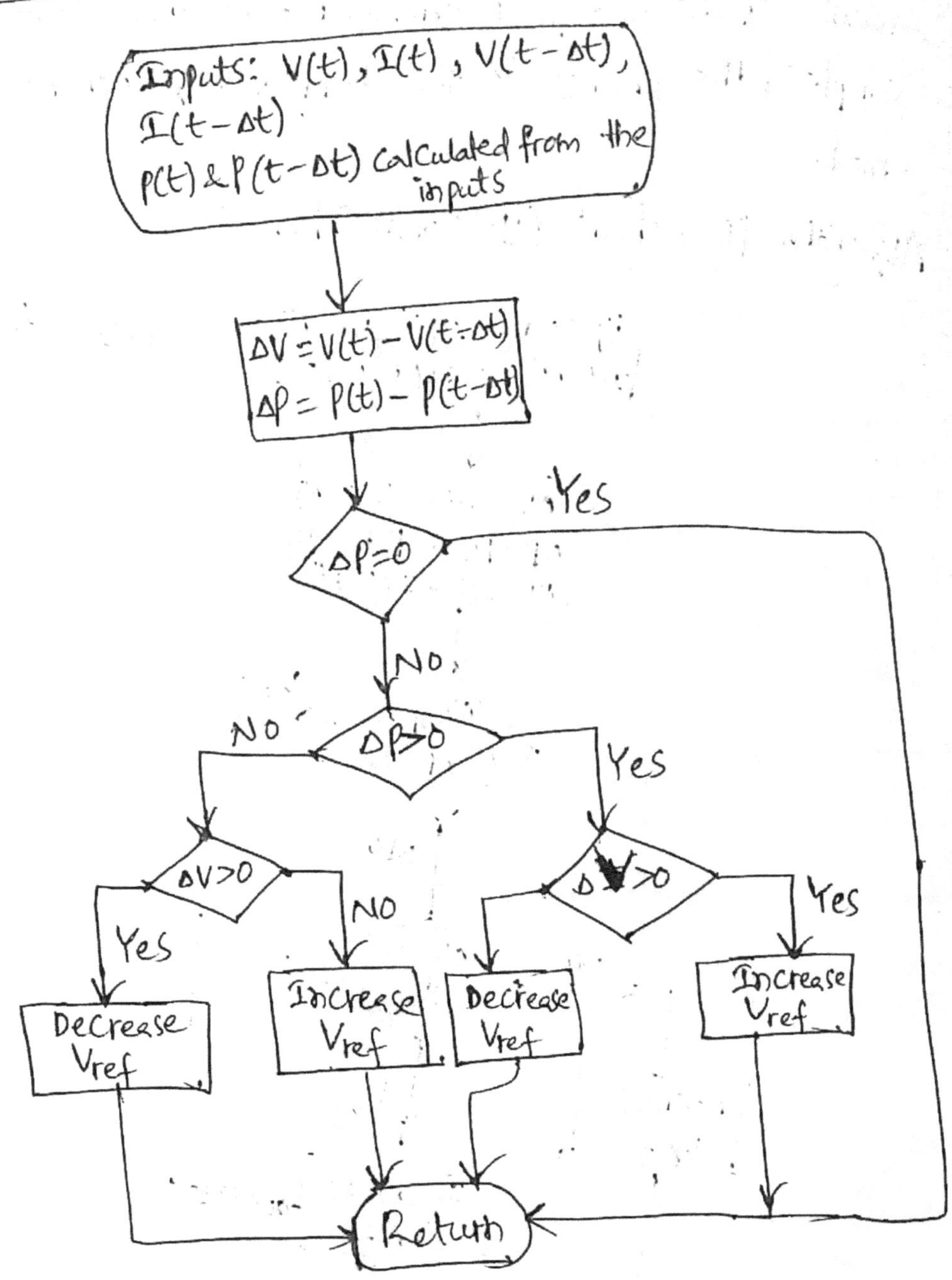

The drawbacks of these techniques are mainly two.
1) They can easily lose track of the MPP if the irradiation
changes rapidly. In case of step changes they track
the MPP very well, because the change is instantaneous
& the curve doesn't keep on changing. However, when

the irradiation changes following a slope, the curve in which the algorithms are based changes continuously with the irradiation. So the changes in the voltage & current are not only due to perturbation of the voltage. As a consequence it is not possible for the algorithms to determine whether the change in power is due to its own voltage increment or due to the change in the irradiation.

2) The other drawback is the oscillations of the voltage & current around the MPP in the steady state. The traditional solution is a trade off: if the increment is small so that the oscillations decrease, then the MPP is reached slowly & vice versa, so a compromise solution has to be found.

Battery Energy Storage Systems

The Role of Energy storage & Benefits :

1) Reduce the need for additional transmission assets
2) provide better integration of renewables into the system.
3) Improve the reliability of electric supply.
4) Increase the efficiency of existing power plant & transmission facilities.

Some of Storage Schemes are :

1) **Battery** : This is storage of electric energy by conversion to chemical energy in batteries. The most common & highly developed is the Lead-acid battery. Large electric energy storage in lead acid batteries or other batteries is not economically feasible. Other battery systems with higher energy to mass ratio's are under development. Currently available & suitable storage batteries have capacities between 40 to 280 Ah.

A storage battery cycle operation consists of a charging process & discharging process.

The amount of energy stored during charging process,

$$P_s = C V_B \ (Wh) \quad , \text{where}$$

C is storage capacity (Ah)

V_B is nominal Battery voltage (V).

The amount of energy recovered from a battery during discharging process, $P_d = V_d I_d \, t_d \ (Wh)$, where

V_d is discharge voltage (V)

I_d is discharge current (A)

t_d is discharge duration (h)

2) Pumped - Hydro Storage

This method is more suitable for large power plants. The suplus energy is used to pump water into high reservoirs during sunny periods or periods of low demands & extraction of power during evening or cloudy periods or periods of high demands by running the stored water through water turbines.

The main limitation of this system is to find sites with suitable topography near solar power plants. Such power plants are mostly located in desert like flat terrains.

3) Cryogenic Storage

The electric energy is directly stored in large underground electrical coils at liquid - helium temperatures of 4K. The electrical resistivity is almost zero.

Most promising Battery technologies

1) Lithium Based
2) Metal - air
3) Redox flow Batteries.
4) Sodium Based

2) <u>Metal – Air</u> : These have gained much attention recently as a possible alternative, due to their extremely high energy density compared to that of other rechargeable batteries as well as the low cost.

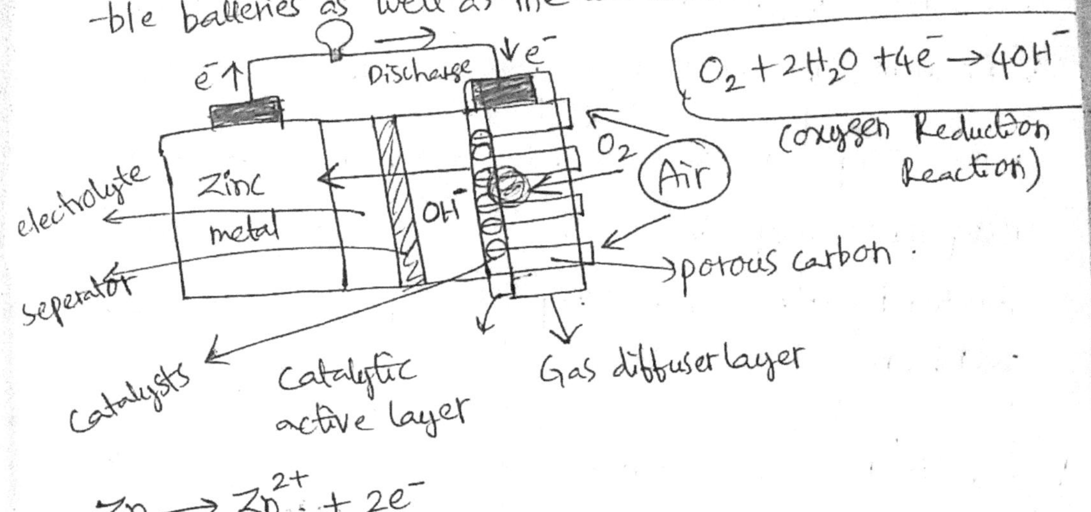

$$Zn \rightarrow Zn^{2+} + 2e^-$$

$$Zn^{2+} + 4OH^- \rightarrow Zn(OH)_4^{2-}$$

$$Zn(OH)_4^{2-} \rightarrow ZnO + H_2O + 2OH^-$$

Zn – air	Li – air
1) Stable towards moisture, can be assembled outside of glove box.	Not moisture stable, increasing cost & manufacturing complexity
2) Zn metal & aqueous electrolytes are inexpensive	Lithium & non aqueous electrolytes are costly
3) Technology is closer to or already in practical applications	Still in research phase
4) Poor reversibility of reactions	Reversible reactions
5) Low life cycle	Low life cycle
6) Low operating potential	Highest operating potential

Redox flow Batteries : The redox flow cell or Battery is an electrochemical system that stores energy in two solutions containing different redox couples (electroactive species)

Vanadium : The electrolyte containing the active vanadium redox couples in sulfuric acid sol^n is circulated in two independent loops through the electrode compartments divided by a microporous seperator ot an ion conducting membrane

$$VO_2^+ + 2H^+ + e^- \longleftrightarrow VO^{2+} + H_2O$$
$$V^{2+} \longleftrightarrow V^{3+} + e^-$$

Advantages :
1) power is determined by the number of cells in the stack & the size of the electrodes which the energy capacity storage is determined by the concentration & volume of the electrolyte.

2) High efficiency
3) Long cycle lifetime in deep charge / discharge.
4) Easy increase of capacity
5) Normal temperature operation.
6) Can be both electrically recharged & mechanically refueled
7) Low cross - contamination of the two half-cell electrolytes.

Drawbacks :
1) Low energy density 20-30 Wh L^{-1}
2) Materials costs represent a fundamental driver of applicability of these systems.

1) Lithium-ion Battery

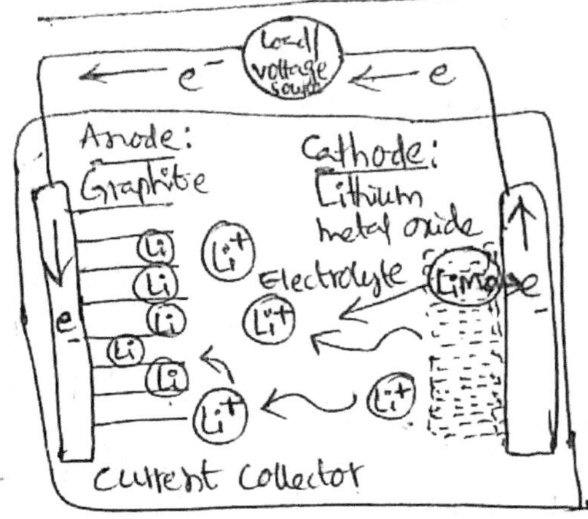

Cathode: Lithium metal oxide

$$LiMO_2 \longleftrightarrow Li_1 - xMO_2 + xLi^+ + xe^-$$

Anode: Graphite or lithium titanate

$$xLi^+ + xe^- + 6C \longleftrightarrow Li_xC_6$$

Electrolyte: Lithium Salt

e.g. $LiPF_6$ in organic solvent.

Advantages

1) High energy & power density
2) Low self-discharge rate
3) Light weight
4) Small size, longer life, low maintenance
5) Quick charging (typically 1-2 hours)

Key end user groups:

1) Military   2) Medical   3) Data collection   4) Heavy duty Cordless

5) Telecom & Data communication

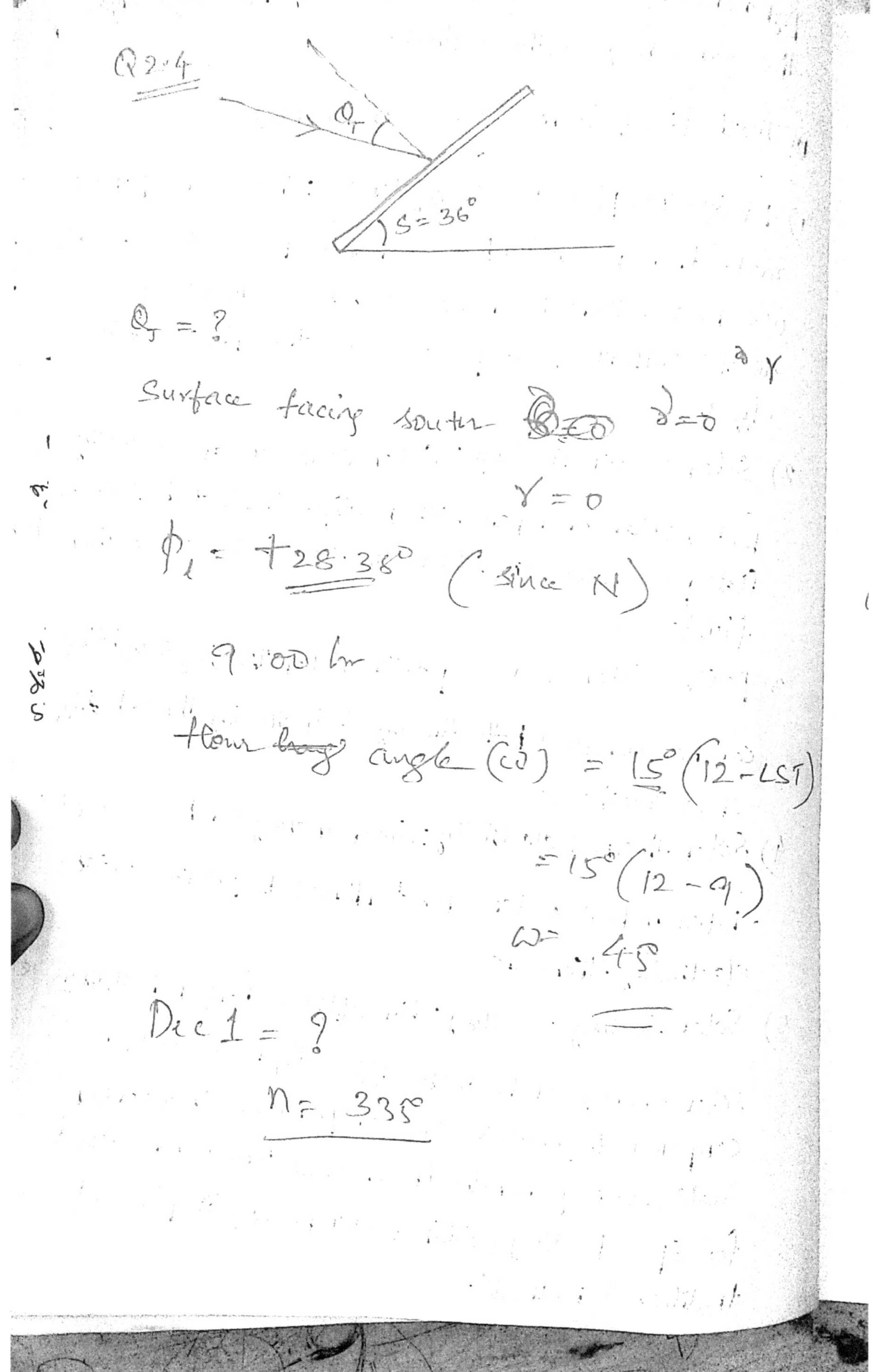

Q2.4

$s = 36°$

$Q_T = ?$

Surface facing south $\Rightarrow$ $\gamma = 0$

$\gamma = 0$

$\phi_l = +28.38°$ (since N)

9:00 hr

Hour angle $(\omega) = 15°(12 - LST)$

$= 15°(12 - 9)$

$\omega = 45°$

Dec 1 = ?

$n = 335$

$$\cos\theta_T = \sin\delta \sin(\phi - s) + \cos\delta \cos w \cos(\phi - s)$$

$$\delta = 23.45 \sin\left[\frac{360}{365}(284 + n)\right]$$

$$\delta = ?$$

$$\cos\theta_T =$$

Biomass $\xrightarrow[\text{Digestion}]{\text{Anaerobic}}$ Biogas

Throughout the process of anaerobic digestion, large organic polymers that make up Biomass are broken down into smaller molecules by chemicals & microorganisms. Upon completion of the anaerobic digestion process, the Biomass is converted into Biogas, namely CO_2 & methane, as well as, digestate & wastewater.

Flow chart

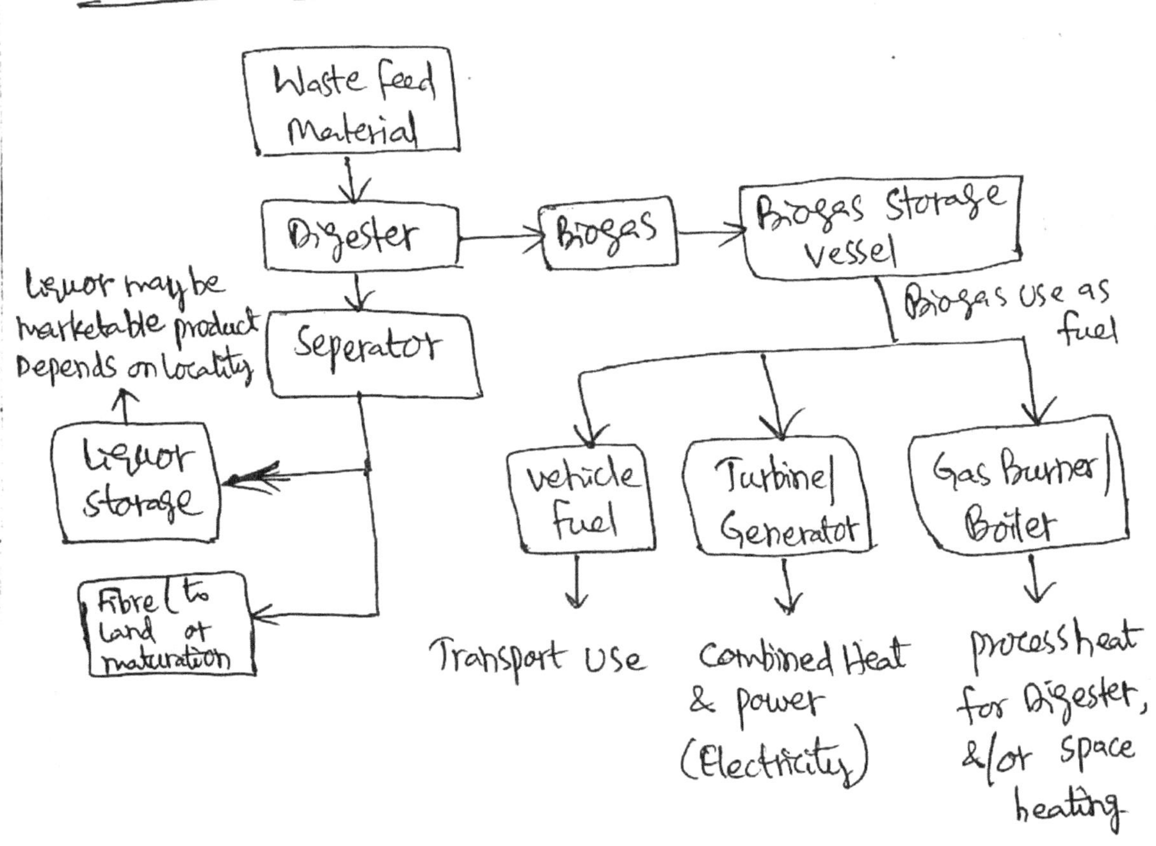

UNIT-V Bio-mass

Anaerobic digestion: It is an expensive process to complete. It requires continual introduction of large quantities of feed stock in order for the process to work efficiently. This is one of the reasons that it generates large quantities of methane gas as the food waste decomposes. That methane gas is not only highly combustible, methane gas is one of the most potent green house gasses on the planet. Further, as this gas builds up within the system, the pressures within make it highly explosive & a safety hazard that must be monitored closely.

Additionally, as the compost is broken down by anaerobic digestion, it creates a sludge-like material that is even more difficult to break down. This requires time & considerable amounts of energy to accomplish. As a matter of fact, it can take up to a year before an anaerobic composter can fully breakdown the raw material into a viable compost.

Aerobic digestion: The process of aerobic digestion that takes place within in-vessel aerobic composters is very similar to the process that occurs without any human assistance in nature. However, instead of taking place on the forest floor beneath the pitter patter of hooves & the like, the process takes place in a container that is easily monitored & maintained.

As aerobic digestion within the in-vessel composter takes place, the byproducts are simply heat, water & carbon dioxide (CO_2). while CO_2 is green house gas, it is at least $1/20^{th}$ as potent as methane. To minimize the impact on the environment, the CO_2 gas can be safely collected via a gas collection system that will prevent the gas from seeping out into environment.

Naturally one of the most important benefits of aerobic composting is that the heat which is produced during the decomposition process is great enough that it kills harmful bacteria & pathogens within the pile. This is not the heat of Hades or phoenix in July, but rather it ranges between 55F & 140F, & is usually lasts for just a few days or so. which this heat is killing the harmful bacteria, it is also facilitating the growth of beneficial bacteria species including psychrophilic, mesophilic & thermophilic bacteria which thrive at the higher temperature levels.

Types of Biogas digesters

Based on model of Biodigesters

The Biodigesters are available in two designs namely floating dome type or fixed dome type & can be placed vertically or horizontally at site. The vertical design is used at non rocky places where water level is to be

3m or more. The horizontal design is used at the ③ places of rocky area, has mild water table 1.5m or less. In following biodigester design methods, the digestion process is same in both digester but collection method of gas is different each.

| A) Floating Drum digester | B) ~~Fixed Dome type~~ |
Fixed ~~Floating~~ Dome	Floating Drum type
1) Pressure of gas is variable	1) Gas released at constant pressure
2) High maintanance cost	2) Low maintanance cost
3) Capital cost is high	3) Low capital cost
4) overhead space can be utili-zed for other purposes	4) overhead space can't be utilized for other purposes
5) Higher temperature in winter	5) Lower temp. in winter
6) life is more (20–50 yrs)	6) life is less than fixed dome plant (20–30 yrs)
7) Needs more excavation work	7) needs less excavation work
8) steel gas holder not required	8) Steel gas holder is a must

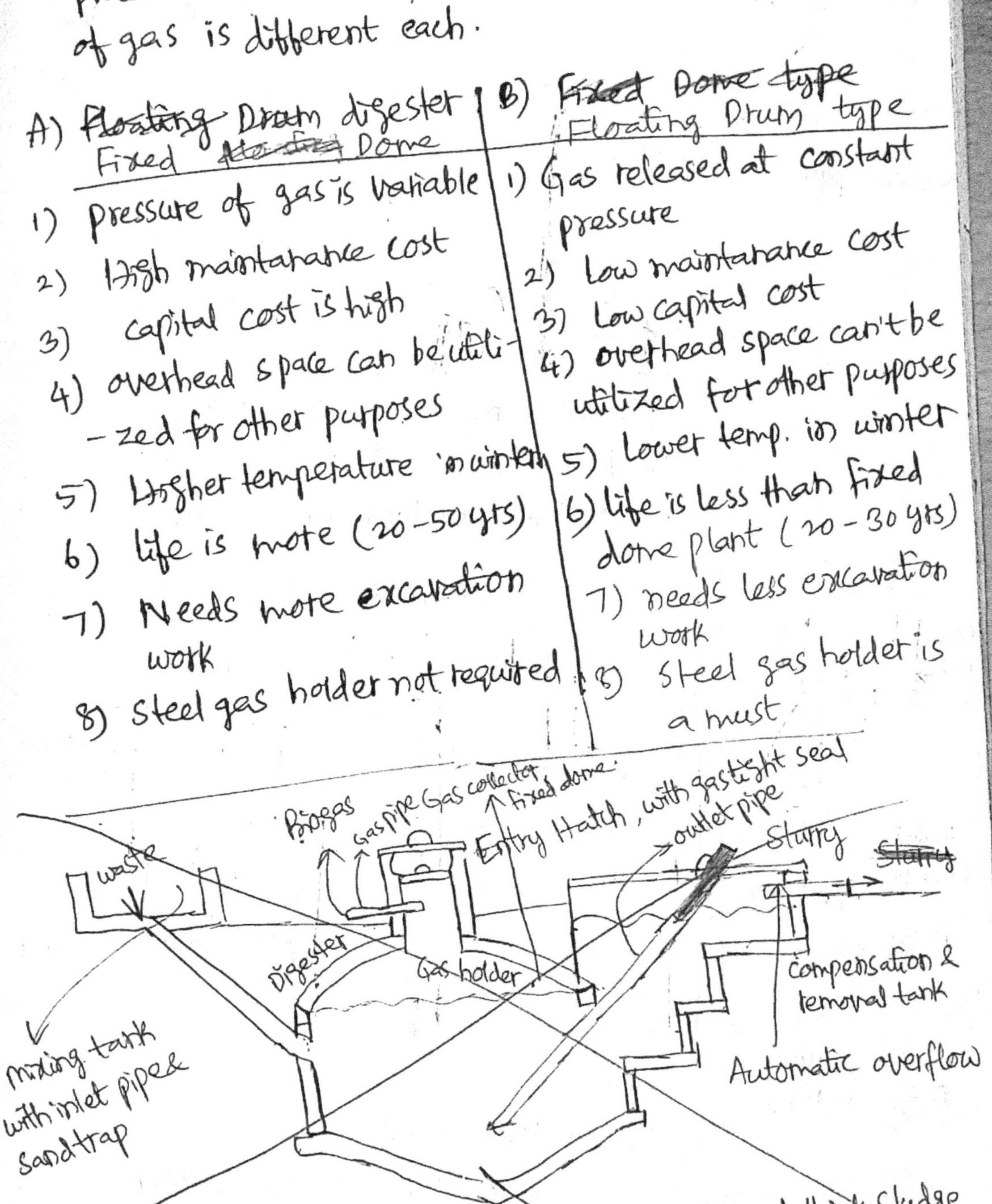

Fixed-dome plants.
Ex: Janta module of Bio digester.

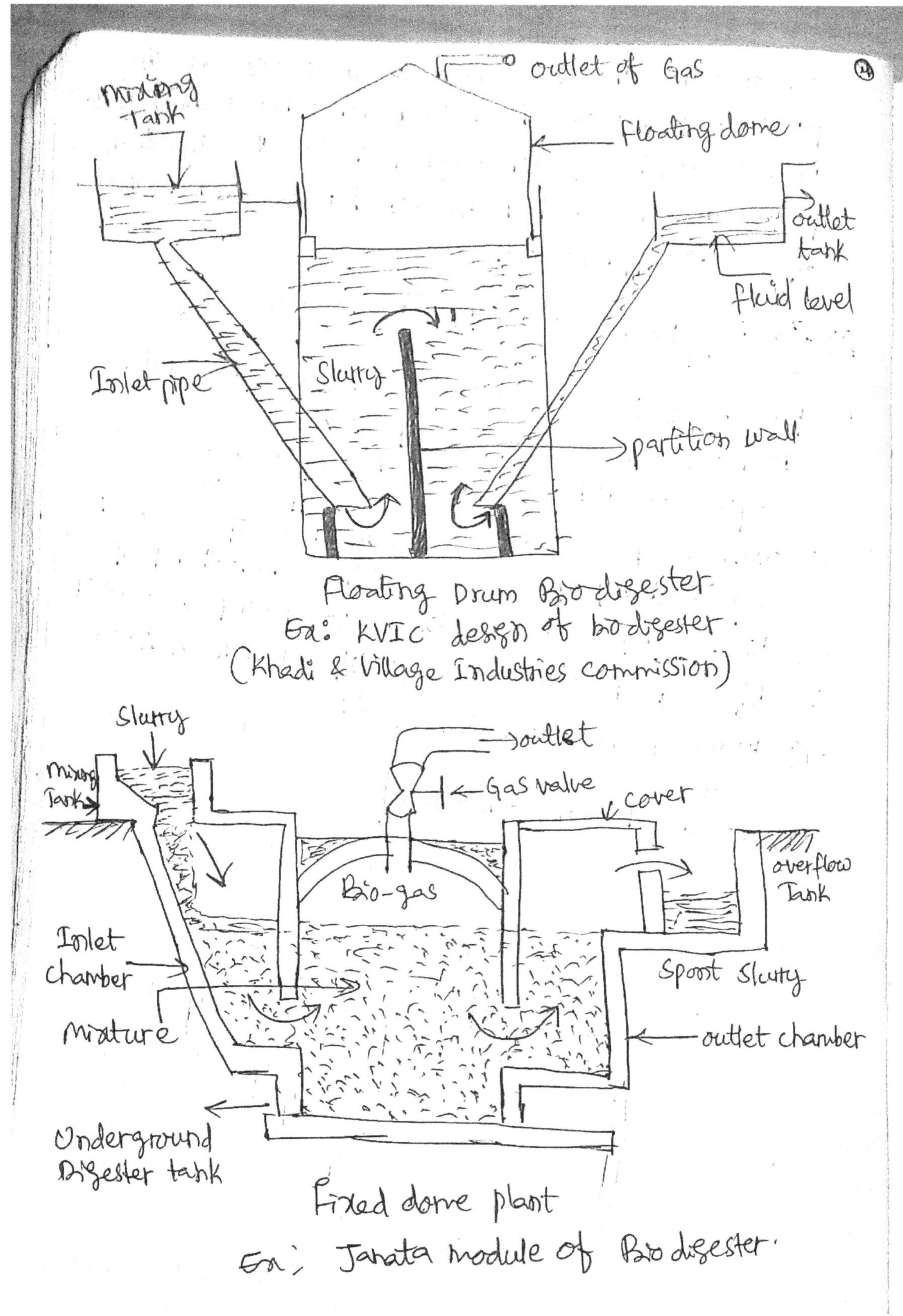

Floating Drum Biodigester
Ex: KVIC design of biodigester.
(Khadi & Village Industries commission)

Fixed dome plant
Ex; Janata module of Biodigester.

Power Generation by Biomass

Biomass power is the electricity production from biomass as a fuel & uses crops residues, wood waste, waste from industries, food waste, animals waste etc. A bio-power technology, fuel cells & boiler or by other methods. The product from different conversion route is further utilized by several processes to generate bio power. The Rankine cycle (for steam turbine) or Brayton cycle (for gas turbine) is used by majority of bio power plants. Steam is a most common working fluid in Rankine cycle because of its many desirable characteristics & can be used in both open & closed system. & ~~shown in fig~~

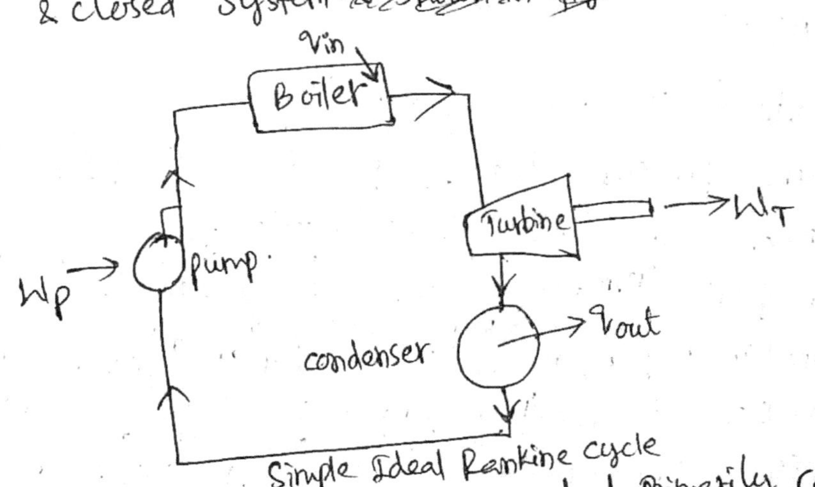

Simple Ideal Rankine cycle

Since biomass fuel is composed of primarily carbon, Hydrogen & oxygen, it is a good substitute for the plants fired by coal or natural gas. In biomass fired steam power plants the biomass is fed from bunker through pulverizer in order to reduce the size of particle from for fast burning during suspension in air. The pulverized fuel mixed with primary air is fed through burner in the furnace & gets burned. The complete combustion of this partially burned fuel takes place in the boiler compartment

with the injection of secondary air. The efficiency of cyc[?]
is improved by providing super heater & economizer in
the circuit. The steam produced in the boiler is used to
run the steam turbine coupled with generator to produce
electricity.

Properties of Biogas as fuel for IC Engines
~~Biogas is the product of fermen~~

Different Reaction phases in a Digester

1) Hydrolysis:
2) Acidogenesis:
3) Acetogenesis
4) Methanogenesis

Factors affecting the Biogas generation

1) Temperature & pressure (Rate of gas production↑ as Temp↑)
2) Solid concentration & loading rate (Under loading & overloading reduces the biogas production)
3) Retention period (The longer Retention period needs larger size digester & it allows more complete digestion of feed)
4) pH value or Hydrogen ion concentration (Ideal pH value is blw 7-8. but can go up or down by a further 0.5.
5) Nutrients concentration (The major nutrients required by the bacteria in the digester are N_2, P, S, C, H_2 & O_2 to accelerate anaerobic digestion rate)
6) Supplementary Nutrients
7) Harmful materials (The presence of some materials like Cu, Cr, Ni reduces fermentation rate.
8) Water content (This should be about 90% of the weight of the total contents)
9) Reaction period (Under optimum condition 80-90% of total gas production is obtained within a period of 3-4 weeks)
10) Stirring or Agitation of the content of digester (If not stirred the slurry will tend to settle down & form a hard scum on the surface which prevents release of biogas.
11) Harmful effects of chemical fertilizers. left over of a biogas plant is an excellent fertilzer for the plants & can be used instead of chemical fertilizer. For example nitrate of soda, the plant take much of nitrate but not soda which when combines with ... makes soil hard.
12) Gas Collection

Advantages of Biomass energy

1) Biomass used as a fuel reduces need for fossil fuels for the production of heat, steam, & electricity for residual, industrial & agricultural use.

2) Biomass is always available & can be produced as a renewable resource.

3) Biomass fuel from agricultural wastes may be a secondary product that adds value to agricultural crop.

4) Growing Biomass crops produce oxygen & use up carbon dioxide.

5) The use of waste materials reduce landfill disposal & makes more space for everything else.

6) CO_2 which is released when Biomass fuel is burned is taken in by plants.

7) Less money spent on foreign oil.

Disadvantages

1) Agricultural wastes will not be available if the basic crop is no longer grown

2) Additional work is needed in areas such as harvesting methods.

3) Land used for energy crops maybe in demand for other purposes, such as farming, conservation, housing, resor or agricultural use.

4) Some biomass conversion projects are from animal waste & are relatively small & therefore are limited

5) Research is needed to reduce the costs of production. Biomass based fuels.

6) In some cases. it is major cause of pollution.

Biogas Utilization for cooking

Biogas can be produced on a very small scale for household use, mainly for cooking & water heating or on larger industrial scale where it can either be burnt in power generation devices.

The feed stock; i.e animal dung or sewage, is converted to a slurry with upto 95% water, & for small scale applications fed into a purpose built digester. Digesters come in many forms & sizes, which may range from 1 m³ for a small household unit to some 10⁸ m³ for a typical farm plant & more than 1000 m³ for a large installation.

Biogas for cooking uses following components

1) Manure collection: raw, liquid, slurry, semi solid & solid manure can all be used for biogas production.

2) Anaerobic digester: The digester is the component of the manure management system that optimizes naturally occurring anaerobic bacteria to decompose & treat the manure while producing gas.

3) Effluent storage: The products of the anaerobic digestion of manure in digesters are biogas & effluent. The effluent is a stabilized organic soln that has value as a fertilizer & other potential users.

4) Gas Handling: piping, gas pump or blower; gas meter; pressure regulator; & condensate drain (s).

5) Gas use: a cooker or Boiler.

NOTE: For applications on a larger scale, feedstocks such as sewage sludge from waste water treatment plants, wet agricultural residues & the organic fraction of munici- pal solid waste (MSW) can be collected & used.

 Biogas can be used for all applications designed for natural gas, given a certain upgrading of its quality. Upgrading can be done to a level compatible with natural gas ('green gas') by cleaning (removal of H_2S, ammonia & some hydrocarbons from the biogas) & by increasing the methane share (by removing the CO_2)

Environmental benefits of Biogas

1) Create renewable & clean energy. You'll be less dependent on fossil fuels & help preserve precious natural resources.

2) Reduced greenhouse gas emissions. methane is believed to be a significant cause of climate change. By capturing methane & using it as fuel, you are preventing it from releasing into the atmosphere.

3) Reduced contamination of ground water, surface water & other resources

4) The biogas process effectively destroys such harmful pathogens as E-coli & M.avium paratuburculosis.

5) waste is converted into high quality fertilizer.

6) A biodigester can't only create fuel out of manure, but other organic waste such as waste water, slaughter house waste, biodegradable garbage, straw, crop stalks & night soil.

As mentioned earlier, there are four key stages of anaerobic digestion involve hydrolysis, acidogenesis, acetogenesis & methanogenesis. The overall process can be described by the chemical reaction, where organic material such as glucose is biochemically digested into CO_2 & methane by anaerobic microorganisms.

$$C_6H_{12}O_6 \longrightarrow 3CO_2 + 3CH_4$$

1) **Hydrolysis:** In most cases biomass is made up of large organic polymers. For the bacteria in anaerobic digesters to access the energy potential of the material, these chains must first be broken down into their smaller constituent parts. These constituent parts, or monomers such as sugars are readily available to other bacteria. The process of breaking these chains & dissolving the smaller molecules into solutions is called hydrolysis. Therefore, hydrolysis of these high molecular weight polymeric components is the necessary first step in anaerobic digestion.

Complex organic molecules	→ Simple Sugars
	→ Amino Acids
	→ Fatty Acids

2) **Acidogenesis:** The biological process of acidogenesis results in further breakdown of the remaining components by acidogenic bacteria. Here, VFA s (volatile fatty Acids) are created, along with NH_3, CO_2 & H_2S as well as other byproducts.

3) **Acetogenesis:** The third stage of anaerobic digestion is " acetogenesis. Here, simple molecules created through the acedogenesis phase are further digested by acetogenes to produce largely acetic acid, as well as CO_2 & H_2.

4) **Methanogenesis:** The terminal stage of anerobic digestion is the biological process of methanogenesis. Here, methano -gens use the intermediate products of the preceding stages & convert them into methane, CO_2 & H_2O. These components make up the majority of the biogas emitted from the system. Methanogenesis is sensitive to both high & low PH.S & occurs between pH 6.5 & PH 8.

$$CO_2 + 4H_2 \rightarrow CH_4 + 2H_2O$$
$$CH_3COOH \rightarrow CH_4 + CO_2$$

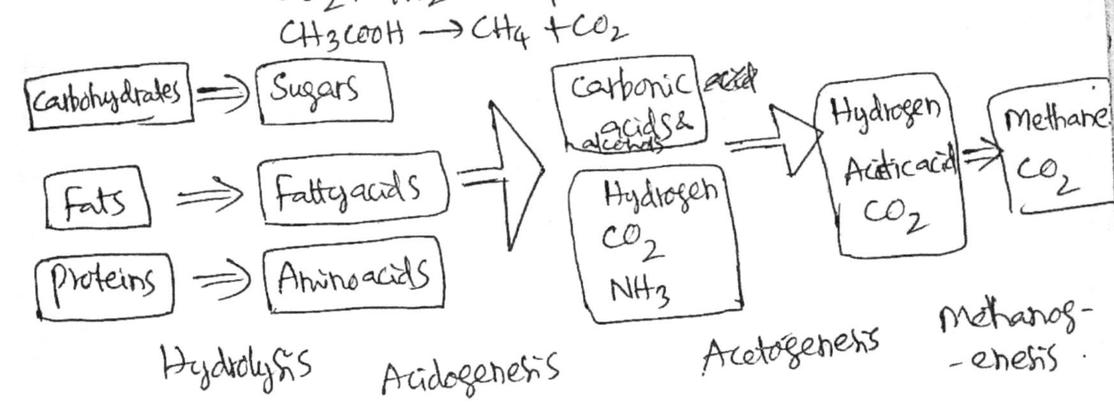

Definitions:

Retention period: It represents the time period for which the fermentable material remains inside the digester. This period ranges from 35 days to 50 days depending upon the climatic conditions & location of the digester.

Slurry: A semi-liquid mixture, typically of fine particles of manure, cement, or coal & water.

Effluent: liquid waste or sewage discharged into a river or sea.

- <u>Manure</u> : Animal dung used for fertilizing land.

6. Geothermal Energy

Geothermal energy is thermal energy generated & stored in the earth. Thermal energy is the energy that determines the temperature of matter. The geothermal energy of the earth's crust originate from the original formation of the planet & from radio active decay of materials.

Resources: The earth's internal thermal energy flows to the surface by conduction at a rate of 44.2 Terawatts, & is (TW) replenished by radioactive decay of minerals at a rate of 30 TW. These power rates are more than double humanity's current energy consumption from all primary sources, but most of this energy flow is not recoverable. In addition to the internal heat flows, the top layer of the surface to a depth of 10 meters (33 ft) is heated by Solar energy during the Summer, & releases that energy & cools during the winter.

A geothermal heat pump can extract enough heat from Shallow ground anywhere in the world to provide home heating, but industrial applications need higher temperatures of deep resources.

Outside of the Seasonal variations, the geothermal gradient of temperatures through the crust is 25-30°C per kilometer of depth in most of the world.

Environmental Considerations

1) Fluids drawn from deep earth carry a mixture of gases, notably CO_2, H_2S, CH_4 & NH_3. These pollutants contribute to global warming, acid rain & noxious smells if released.

2) In addition to dissolved gases, hot water from geothermal sources may hold in solution trace amounts of toxic elements such as mercury, arsenic, boron & antimony. These chemicals precipitate as the water cools, & can cause environmental damage if released.

3) Plant construction can adversely affect land stability & may lead to earthquakes etc.

4) Geothermal power plants can have impacts on both water quality & consumption. Hot water pumped from underground reservoirs often contains high levels of Sulphur, Salt & other minerals.

5) The dinstinction between open & closed loop systems is important with respect to air emissions. In closed loop systems, gases removed from the well are not exposed to the atmosphere & are injected back into the ground after giving up their heat, so air emissions are minimal. In contrast open loop systems emit H_2S, CO_2, NH_3, CH_4 & boron.

Power Generation From Geothermal energy

The basic mechanism for generating electricity from geothermal resources is quite simple. This involves using heat from below the earth's surface to heat water, which is then used to drive a turbine that connects to a generator that generates electricity.

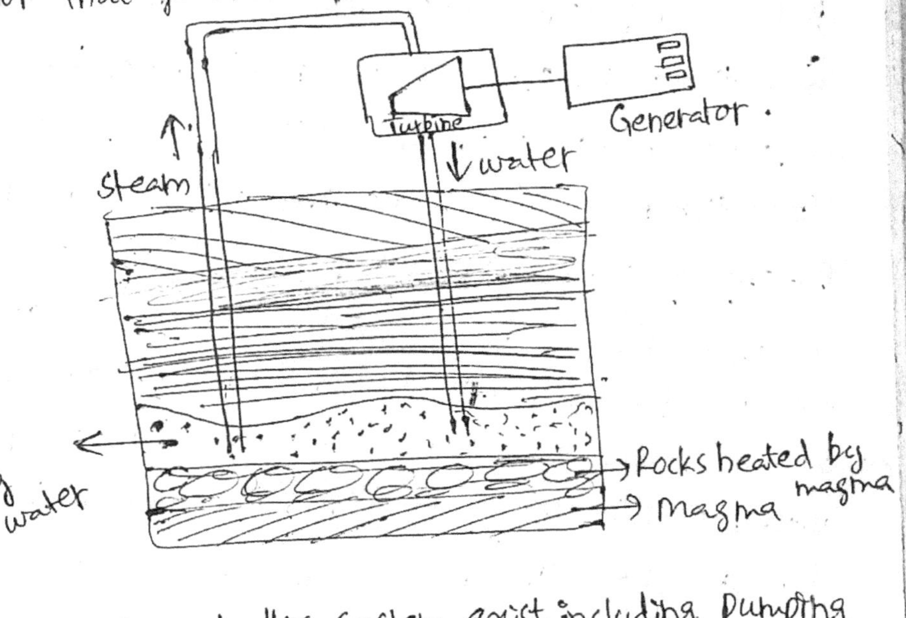

Several variations to this system exist, including pumping up pre-existing heated water or steam from below the earth's surface as the source of water, as well as pumping surface water down to a heated area below the earth's surface where it becomes heated & then pumped up again.

There are several technical setups for generating electricity from geothermal conditions.

1) Dry steam power plants: Here the steam is piped directly from underground wells to the power plant, where it is directed into a turbine / Generator unit.

Flash steam power plants: These are most common. They use geothermal reservoirs of water with temperatures greater than 360°F (182°C). This very hot water flows up through wells in the ground under its own pressure. As it flows upward, the pressure decreases & some of the hot water boils into steam. The steam is then seperated from the water & used to power a turbine/Generator. Any leftover water & condensed steam are injected back into the reservoir, making this a sustainable resource.

Binary cycle power plants: These plants operate on water at lower temperatures of about (107° - 182°C). These plants use the heat from the hot water to boil a working fluid, usually an organic compound with a low boiling point. The working fluid is vaporized in a heat exchanger & used to turn a turbine. The water is then injected back into the ground to be reheated. The water & the working fluid are kept seperated during the whole process, so there are little or no air emissions.

Potential in India

It has been estimated from geological, geochemical, shallow geophysical & shallow drilling data it is estimated that india has about 10,000 MWe of geothermal power potential that can be harnessed for various purposes. Rocks covered on the surface of India ranging in age from more than 4500 million years to the present day & distributed in different geographical units. The rocks comprise of Archean,

proterozoic, Teritary etc, more than 300 hot spring locations
have been identified by Geological Survey of

Types of wells :
____

Geothermal wells also known as geo exchange systems
have 2 basic designs. They are
open looped Systems : (The efficient choice)
______________________ In an open loop system, ground water
is pumped from water well into a heat exchanger located
in a surface dwelling. The water drawn from the earth is
then pumped back into the acquifer through a different well,
or in some cases the same well. Alternatively, the ground
water could be discharged to a surface of water body.
In the heating mode, cooler water is returned to the earth,
while in the cooling mode, warmer water is returned.

aquifer : Underground bed or layer yielding grounda
____
water for wells & springs etc.
dwelling : Housing that someone is living in
____

→ Open loop systems are typically used on rural properties
that have two existing high capacity water wells & are
considered to be the most efficient of the loop systems.
These wells should be approximately 100 feet apart. Ground
water is withdrawn from an aquifer through a supply well
& pumped into the ground source heat pump. Once the
heat pump has removed the energy from water, the dischar-
-ged water is redirected into a second well & back into the
aquifer.

The water from the supply well is used as a heat source in the winter & as a heat sink in the summer. This system allows for maximum efficiency in the heatpump because it absorbs energy directly from water pumped out of the well, rather than relying on a water solution re-circulating through a series of underground looped pipes.

On the other hand, while extremely reliable, open loop systems can face consequences down the road if there is a change in the water supply. Water quality can also be a issue as it can lead to mineral build-up inside the heat pump exchanger & require periodic cleaning.

Closed Loop System : (The cost-effective choice)

The most common loop system available for geothermal installations is the closed loop system. It's extremely reliable, requires little maintanance & generates low operating costs. It also offers three options for installation – Horizontal, vertical or pond/lake loops.

Horizontal Loop : This is the most common type of closed loop system & is most often used in rural & new construction areas owing to the land space needed for installation. A continuous loop of high density geothermal pipe is buried in five to six foot deep trenches. The amount of pipe used is dependent upon building load. The trenches are then backfilled with soil.

Vertical loop: This approach is typically used in urban areas because it requires little land space for installation. A specially designed geothermal driller is used to bore vertical holes in the ground ranging from 180 to 540 feet deep. A typical installation would require about 360 linear feet of 1-1/4" high density geothermal pipe per nominal ton. The pipe is looped within the holes & the holes are then filled with bentonite grout (used as a bond for covering a wall). Vertical installation costs tend to be higher than horizontal & pond/lake installations but they generally require less pipe.

Pond/Lake loop: Similar in costs to horizontal loop systems, this approach can be used on properties that have a nearby lake or pond that is appropriate in size & eight feet deep. A series of 200 to 250 linear feet of 1-1/4" high density geothermal pipe loops are nominal ton are submerged at the bottom of the body of water. Two pipes are then buried in the ground to carry energy from the lake or pond to the house or commercial building.

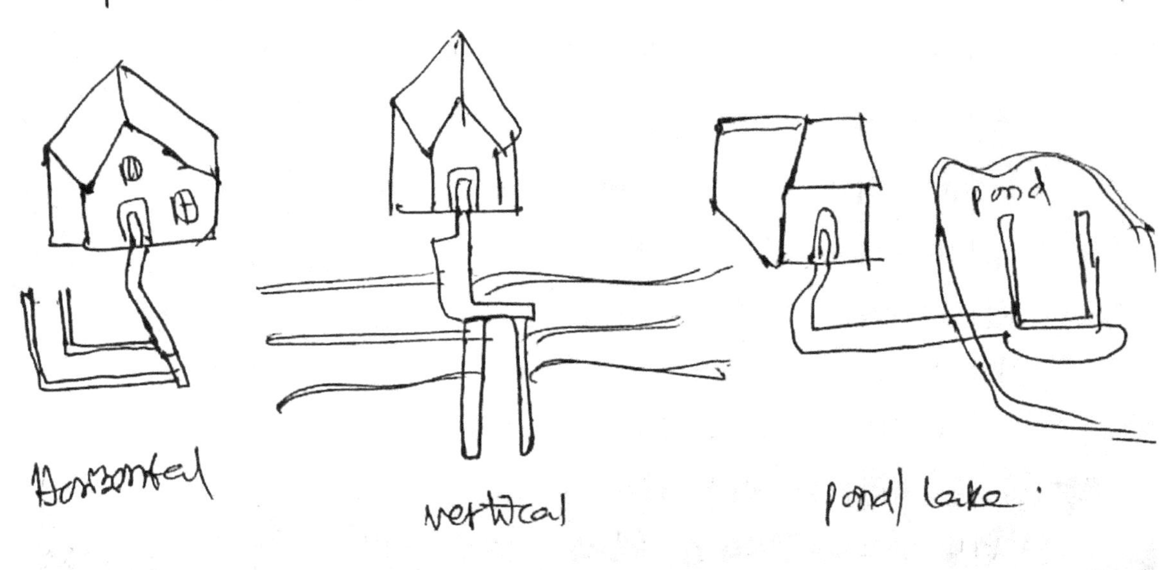

NOTE:

By design, all three closed loop system offer same efficiency. The vertical & pond/lake systems will disturb the least amount of land area. Horizontal & pond/lake systems can be installed in one or two days while vertical systems typically take a week or more to install depending upon drilling conditions.

Methods of Harnessing Geothermal Energy

1) **Direct Geothermal energy.** In areas where hot springs or geothermal reservoirs are near the earth's surface, hot water can be piped in directly to homes or office buildings. Geothermal water is pumped through a heat exchanger, which transfers the heat from the water into the building's heating system. The used water is then

2) **Geothermal Heat pump:** A few feet under the ground, the soil or water remain a constant 50 to 60° F year-round. Just that little bit of warmth can be used to heat or cool homes & offices. Fluid circulates through a series of pipes (called a loop) under the ground or beneath the water of a pond or lake & into a building. In the summer the process is reversed. An electric compressor & heat exchanger pull the heat from the pipes & send it via a duct system throughout the building. In the summer the process is reversed. The pipes draw heat away from the house & carry it to the ground or water outside, where it is absorbed.

3) **Geothermal power plant**
   a) Dry steam plants b) Flash steam plants c) Binary Cycle plants.

Prime movers used in Geothermal conversion system:

Factors to be considered in selecting site for Geothermal power plant

1) Air pollution

2) Visual Quality

3) Vegetation cover: vegetation cover can be damaged during power plant construction in the proposed sites. For reducing the impacts of the plant construction, it it prefered to locate in an area with minimum vegetation cover density

4) Waste water: Distance of the site to the injection & surface discharge areas should be considered.

5) Noise Impacts: Noise is one of the most ubiquitous disturbances to the environment from geothermal development, particularly during the construction & operation phases.

6) Land stability & Subsidence Risk: Subsidence is the motion of a surface as it shifts downwards relative to a datum such as sea-level, it should be taken care.

7) Slope & Surface disturbance: An area with a high slope causes more disturbance to the surface. Thus a power plant site with a low slope is preferable.

8) Geology & Site Stability Risk: Site may be located on the "Lava with phenocryst" & the "Gravel terraces". Mechanical strength of lava formation is greater than that of gravel terraces.

9) Fractures & Natural risk of pipelines: During the project lifetime natural disasters are probable & an appropriate evaluation of those is needed.

10) **Distance to production field :** Distance of the proposed site to the well field is not only important w.r.t cost for pipe but also important as regards environmental degration of the pipeline corridor.

11) **Access Road Required :**

12) **Power Transmission line :** potential impacts from construction are also of interest to local communities & adjecent land owners.

Hydrothermal Systems:

The vapor & hot water forms of geothermal energy are together known as hydrothermal systems & they are the only forms that are commercially available. These systems are classified as

A) **Water dominated fields (liquid dominated fields)**

Hot water fields — Hot water field contains a water reservoir at temperature ranging 50–100°C. Such fields without much steam content can be useful for house heating & agricultural purposes. The temperature gradient in this field is less. The reservoir contains water in the liquid phase below the boiling point of water under pressure. On the surface, there are often thermal springs whose temperature is near the boiling point of water. These fields occur at the depth less than 2km.

Wet steam fields : The wet steam fields contain pressurised water in reservoir at temperature higher than 100°C. When hot water at high pressure is brought to the surface, its pressure is sufficiently reduced & some water will get flashed in to steam & remaining in the form of boiling water. The resulting mixture is a mixture of water & steam. Such fields are suitable for power generation.

B) **Dry steam or vapour dominated fields**

These fields are similar to wet steam fields but ~~heat source is a natural one. This is very advanced technology & it was under~~ heat transfer from the depth is much higher. These reservoirs produce super heated steam at pressure above atmosphere. The permeability of these fields is lower than wet fields. When the well is drilled, upto the reservoir & extraction of fluid starts, a depressed zone is formed at the bottom of the well, that enhances the boiling of water surrounding the rocks. The steam flows through through the dry bottom area & starts expanding & gets cool. But the heat added by surroun- -ding rocks at high temperature keeps the steam at super heated state. The degree of super heating may reach upto 100°C.

Classification of Geothermal Resources

Geothermal resources are classified on the basis of enthalpy as temperature alone is not sufficient to define the useful energy contents of a steam & water mixture.
They are classified:

a) **High Enthalpy Resources**: There are places in the earth where earth's heat flow is sufficiently high & generates steam or water & at temperature around $180°C - 200°C$. These resources are available in shallow rocks & suitable for electricity generation.

b) **Medium Enthalpy Resources**: These resources generate steam & water between $100°C - 180°C$, & are suitable for electricity generation by using binary cycle as well as for thermal applications.

c) **Low Enthalpy Resources**: These resources generate water below $100°C$, & are suitable for thermal heating by using hot water in the field of space heating, agricultural, industrial process etc.

Basic technologies According to Resource temperature

Reservoir Temperature	Reservoir fluid	Common use	Technology commonly used
High Temperature or high Enthalpy $> 180 - 200°C$	Water or Steam	Power Generation / Direct use	Flash Steam; Combined (Flash & Binary); Direct fluid use; Heat exchangers heat; pumps
Intermediate Temperature or medium enthalpy $100 - 180°C$	water	Power Generation / Direct Use	Binary cycle Direct fluid use; Heat exchangers; Heat pumps
Low temperature or low enthalpy $50 - 100°C$	water	Direct use	Direct fluid use; Heat exchangers; Heat pumps

Turbines Used for Geothermal power Generation

1) Steam turbine : It is used in petro thermal geothermal power plant & Flashed Steam geothermal power plant.

2) Gas Turbine : It is used in Binary liquid dominated geothermal power plant.

~~Tidal~~ 7. Ocean Energy

Site Requirements for power Generation from Tides

1) The presence of tidal pattern is not alone sufficient to qualify it as a place for tidal power plant setup. The difference b/w flood tide & ebb tide must be minimally of the order of 4.6m or above that.

2) The volume of water moving around during the tide or the cubature of the tidal flow is an important factor which determines the suitability of a site.

3) Wave actions as well as storms are very destructive in nature & hence the site for the tidal power plant should be well protected from these natural agents, otherwise the cost of embankment would be unreasonably high & make the project financially unfeasible.

4) The site shouldn't interrupt the flow of normal shipping traffic which passes through the estuary otherwise it will interrupt the economic cycle of the region.

5) It should be possible to construct a barrage which stores the maximum quantity of water with minimum cost of construction.

6) There are also several other factors such as suitability to marine environment, silt index of water etc.

Embankment: An artificial bank raised above the immediately surro-unding land to redirect or prevent flooding by a river, lake or sea.

The Tidal & Wave Energy

Basic Terminology

1) Tide: The tides are vertical rise of fall of ocean water occurs periodically. The amplitude of tides covers a wide range from 25 cm to 10 m & is repeated in 12 hr 25 minute.

2) Ebb tide: Tide associated with decrease level of water (lowest tide); Flood Tide: The rising of water level from low tide to high tide.

3) Tidal Current: It is the to & fro motion of water in horizontal direction because of change in Tidal level. The tidal currents move with the speed of 1.8 km/sec to 18 km/sec

4) Tidal range: It is the difference b/w consecutive high tide & low tide water & is represented by letter 'R'.

Tidal Energy & its conversion:

Tidal energy is extremely site specific & requires mean tidal range greater than 4 meters as well as favourable topographical conditions. The tides carry huge amount of energy in the moving water & this energy can be extracted from tides by creating a basin behind a dam (known as barrage). Tidal barrages, built across suitable estuaries are designed to extract energy from the rise & fall of the tides, using turbine located in the water route in the barrages. The potential energy stored in the water of the basin beca-use of difference in the water level across the barrage after the tide goes back, is converted into kinetic energy, as the water passes through the turbine placed in the tunnel,

to be brought to the shore & positioning of ships at
water depths of 2km are likely to be problems.

Heat exchanger: Seperates two different fluids from
mixing. Seperating ammonia from Sea water. At top of
heat exchanger that are called Evapourators whats
coming out is high pressure Ammonia vapour. So the once

b) Land Based plant: These are built on land & have the
advantages over floating plants that no power transmission
cable is required to bring the power to shore, & mooring cost
is avoided. These plants are located at coast where deep
water conditions are available within 2-3km distance from
shore. However the length of cold water pipe is more
as it has to cross the Surface zone & then follow the
Seabed untill the depth reaches approx. 800-1000 mts. Therefore
greater friction losses & greater warming of the cold water
before it reaches the heat exchanger, therefore lower
the efficiency.

c) self mounted plant

D) Grazing plant.

for utilizing it directly for power generation, it needs a secondary fluids like ammonia, propane etc. which can evapourate at this low temperature & get condensed in the condenser after expanding in the turbine. The following fig. shows working cycle of heat engine operating at surface temperature, T_s (hot source) & at deep temperature, T_B (cold sink) using secondary fluids. To produce electricity we either use working fluid with a low boiling temperature i.e. Ammonia, Freon's etc, or warm surface sea water by depressurising it to turn into vapour. The thermal efficiency of OTEC plant is 2-3% after considering all losses & pump work.

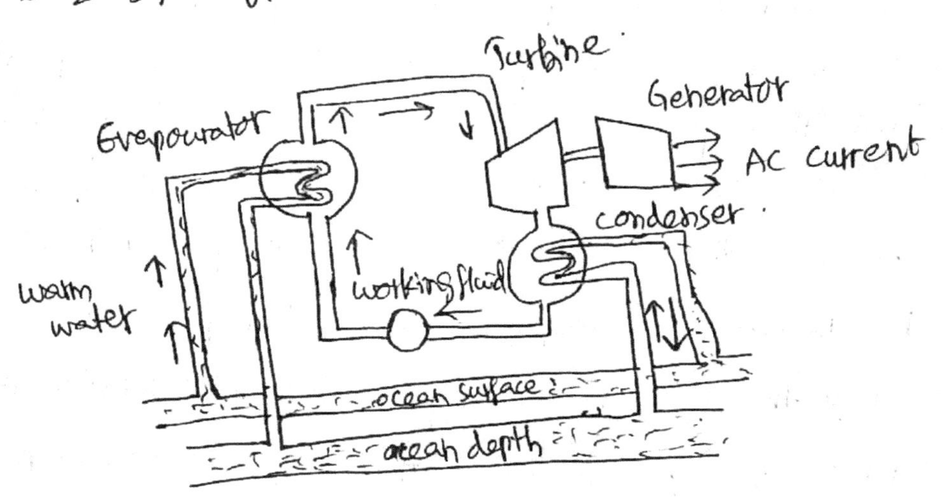

Location of OTEC System :

A) **Floating plant** : These are located at a distance of from shore on the floating platform & preferred at places having deep sea 10-15 km from the shore. These plants have the advantage that the cold water pipe suspended vertically is shorter, reaching directly down to the cold resource, but have the disadvantages that the power generated has to

Working principle of OTEC plant :

The main objective of OTEC is to utilize the solar energy trapped by the ocean into useable energy. This kind of energy is found in tropical oceans where the 20°c difference between top surface & at the depth is sufficient to provide thermal energy continuously, to be utilized for useful work.

The principle of OTEC is that there is a temperature difference ~~we~~ b/w water at the bottom of the sea & the ~~bottom of the sea~~ water at the top. This temperature difference can be used to operate a heat engine. Most of the radiation is being absorbed at the surface layer of water & become lighter. The mixing b/w hot water & cold water is prevented because no thermal convection occurs b/w hot & cold water layer. This means that the surface layer will act as a source & cold layer act as a sink. Therefore it is essential to connect the reversible engine b/w source & cold sink to produce work, that can be converted into required applications.

OTEC plants are most suitable for islands around the tropical region of the east pacific ocean. Because this region has greater temperature differences, which is about 24°c. The carnot efficiency of reversed heat engine operating at surface temperature, T_S (hot source) & at deep temperature, T_B (cold sink) is given as

$$\eta_{carnot} = \frac{T_S - T_B}{T_S}$$

→ As the warm water temperature is not sufficient

which inturn rotates the blades of it & finally conversion of this mechanical energy takes place into electrical energy by coupled generator

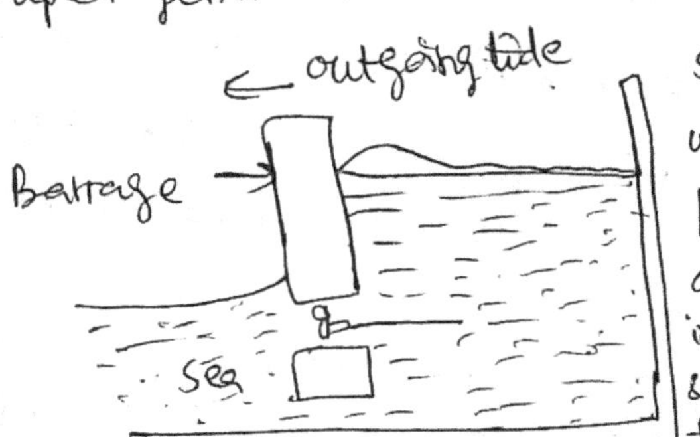

The view of tidal water stored in basin of area 'A', upto height R, behind the barrage after one tide is over. The trapped water inside basin having mass 'm', & assuming that all water falls through $\frac{R}{2}$; i-e centre of gravity through the turbine.

let at any time 't' the range is 'h' & drop in tidal range is 'dh' in time duration 'dt' during the flow from high side to low side.

The work (dE) is equal to change in potential energy due to change in mass (dm) of water is:

$$dE = g \times dm \times h$$

$$dE = + g \, \rho \, A h \, dh \qquad (\because \; m = \rho A h$$
$$dE = m g \, dh \qquad\qquad\quad dm = \rho A \, dh)$$

$$E = \int_{0}^{R} dE \qquad \Rightarrow \text{The Total energy obtained from emptying the basin.}$$

$$E = \int_{0}^{R} m g \, dh = m g$$

The maximum potential energy available per tidal cycle for single effect scheme is given as

$$E = mg\frac{R}{2}$$

$$m = \rho A R$$

$$E = \rho g \, A \frac{R^2}{2} = W A \frac{R^2}{2}$$

For double effect scheme; Energy per tidal cycle is

$$E = W A R^2 ,$$

The capacity of basin is $= A \times R$ where

  $W =$ specific weight of water
  $\rho =$ density of water.
  $A =$ Area of basin.
  $R =$ Height of water level in the basin above low tide level.

The next cycle will be repeated & if the tidal cycle duration is 'T', then the average potential that can be extracted.

$$\bar{E} = \frac{E}{T}$$

Utilization of Tidal Energy in Single-basin arrangement

1) <u>Ebb-Generation</u> : As shown in fig. in simple tidal scheme water is filled in the basin through sluice during incoming high tide (during flood) without power generation. When the water in the basin is filled up to crust level or near to high water level, the sluice gate gets closed. The water is trapped behind the barrage by closing the gate & it passes (outgoing ebb) through the turbine from the basin into ocean through turbine to generate power. This power is available for short duration.

2) **Flood Generation:** In this arrangement, the sluice gates are not provided in the barrages & incoming flood tide rotates the turbine runner to generate power as the high pressure water enters through the turbine passage.

Wave Energy :

This energy is in the form of motion of water particles & can be converted to mechanical form or some other form by using wave machines. The wave energy is difficult to collect because of wide fluctuation in frequency & amplitude at any point. There are no. of wave energy offshore systems used to extract the wave energy via an interface that transfers the force of wave to mechanical motion.

The wave energy systems are constructed with flexible moorings & transmission cable as the devices are floating type & float near or at the surface of ocean to extract maximum power of the incident wave. The most promising devices to meet the demand of local coastal areas are given below.

A) **Hose pump** : It consists of elastomeric hose, which reduces its volume when stretched. The system floats near the surface by means of float. While oscillating with the surface waves, the water gets pressurised in the hose & is fed to the turbine runner placed at bottom of hose through non turnable valve.

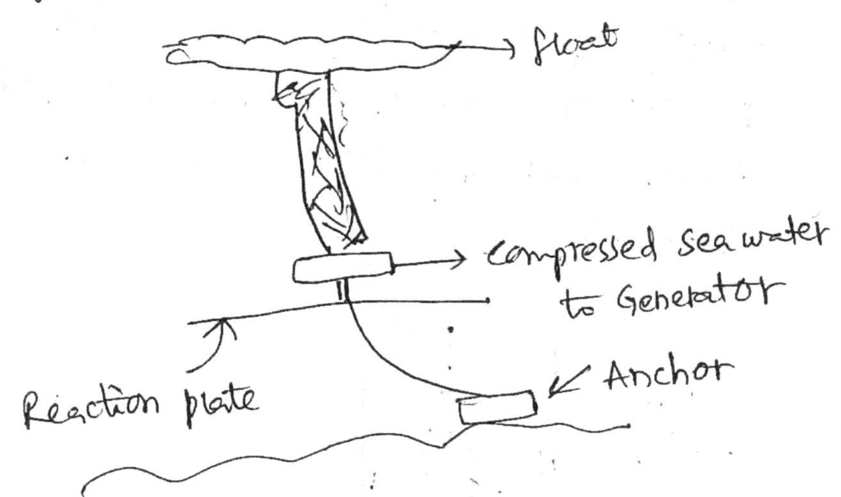

B) **pelamis** : This device is intended for general deployment offshore & is designed to use technology already available in the offshore industry. It is composed of hollow cylindrical sections joined by hinged joint. The energy is extracted by hydraulic rams as waves run down the length of the device & actuate the joints that drive hydraulic motor via an energy soothing system

c) Oscillating water column device: The fig. below
shows the device. In this oscillating column of water
pushes the air above the water column & these
oscillations of air transferred to the air turbine connected
to it. The atmospheric air moves inside the column
when waves fall & goes out when waves rise. The
velocity of air oscillating can be further increased
by decreasing the cross section area of the channel
through which air passes the turbine & becomes an
added advantage.

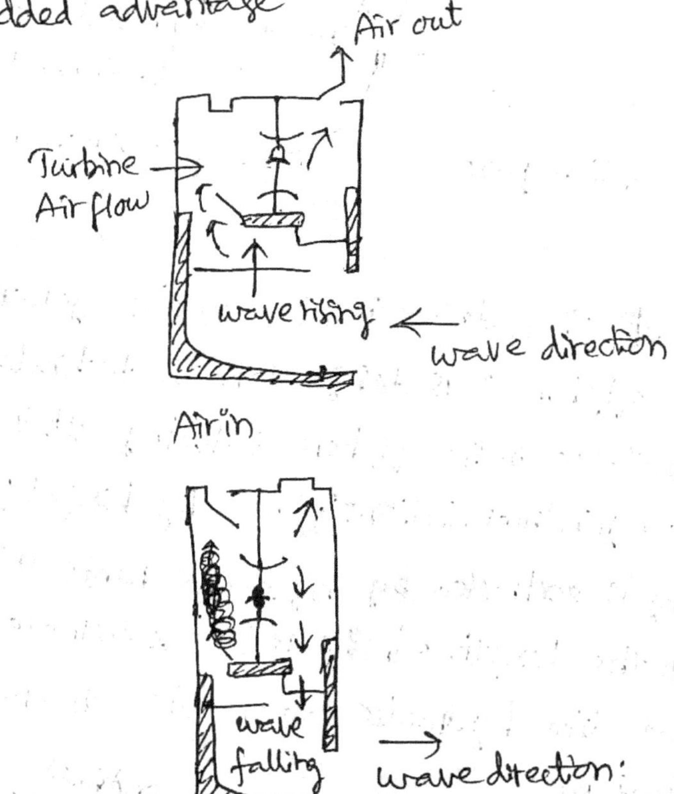

Mini-Hydel power plants (~~30MW~~)
(100 KW - 1 MW)

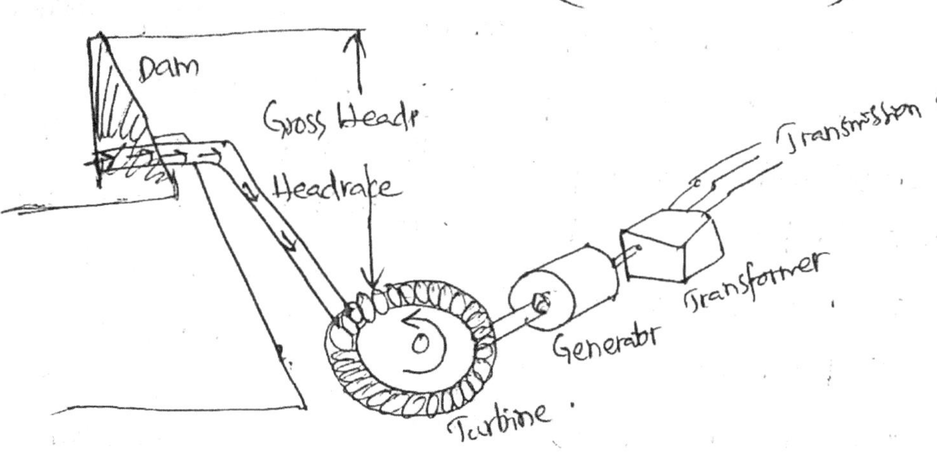

Hydropower systems use the energy in flowing water to produce electricity or mechanical energy. The water flows via channel or penstock to a waterwheel or turbine where it strikes the bucket of the wheel, causing the shaft of the waterwheel or turbine to rotate. When generating electricity, the rotating shaft, which is connected to an alternator or generator, converts the motion of the shaft into electrical energy.

Classification of small hydro power by size

Small-Hydro	1–15 MW → Usually feeding into a grid
Mini Hydro	100 KW – 1 MW → either stand alone or more often feeding the grid.
Micro Hydro	few kWs – 100 KW → Usually provided power for a small community or rural industry
Pico Hydro	few hundred watts – 5 KW.

Economical Considerations - Cost Reduction

The major cost of a scheme is for site preparation & the capital cost of equipment. In general, unit cost decreases with a larger plant & with high heads of water. It could be argued that small-scale hydro technology doesn't bring with it the advantages of "economy of scale", but many costs normally associated with larger hydro schemes have been "designed out" or "planned out" of mini hydro systems to bring the unit cost in line with bigger schemes.

This includes such innovations as:

1) Using run-of-the river schemes where possible - this does away with the cost of an expensive dam for water storage.

2) Locally manufactured equipment where possible & appropriate.

3) Use of HDPE (plastic) penstocks where appropriate.

4) Electronic load controller - allow the powerplant to be left unattended, thereby reducing labour costs, & introduce useful by-products such as battery charging or water heating as pump loads for surplus power;

5) Using an existing infrastructure, for example, a canal which serves an irrigation scheme.

6) Siting of power close to village to avoid expensive high voltage distribution equipment such as transformer.

7) Using pumps as Turbines - in some circumstances standard pumps can be used 'in reverse' as turbines; this reduces costs, delivery time & makes for simple installation & maintenance.

8) Using motors as generators - as with the PAT idea, motors can be run 'in reverse' & used as generators; pumps are usually purchased with a motor fitted & the whole unit can be used as a turbine/Generator set.

9) Use of local materials for civil works.

10) Use of community labour.

11) Good planning for a high plant factor & well balanced load pattern.

12) Self-cleaning intake screens - this is a recent innovation which is fitted to the intake weir & prevents stones & silt from entering the headrace canal;

References

1) Non Conventional Energy Sources by G.D. Roy